Earth
Might
Be
Fair

Edited by

IAN G. BARBOUR

Carleton College

Earth
Might
Be
Fair

Reflections on Ethics,

Religion,

and Ecology

Prentice-Hall, Inc., Englewood Cliffs, New Jersey

To
HAROLD K. SCHILLING

Stanzas from Clifford Bax, "Turn Back, O Man,"
used by permission of A. D. Peters.

Library of Congress Catalog Card Number: 73–167916

Printed in the United States of America

ISBN:
C   0–13–222687–1
P   0–13–222679–0

10 9 8 7 6 5 4 3 2

PRENTICE-HALL INTERNATIONAL, INC.,   *London*
PRENTICE-HALL OF AUSTRALIA, PTY. LTD.,   *Sydney*
PRENTICE-HALL OF CANADA, LTD.,   *Toronto*
PRENTICE-HALL OF INDIA PRIVATE LIMITED,   *New Delhi*
PRENTICE-HALL OF JAPAN, INC.,   *Tokyo*

Contents

Turn back, O man, forswear thy foolish ways.
Old now is earth, and none may count her days;
Yet thou, her child, whose head is crowned with flame,
Still wilt not hear thine inner God proclaim:
"Turn back, O man, forswear thy foolish ways!"

Earth might be fair and all men glad and wise.
Age after age their tragic empires rise,
Built while they dream, and in that dreaming weep;
Would man but wake from out his haunted sleep,
Earth might be fair, and all men glad and wise.

Clifford Bax

IAN G. BARBOUR

1

Introduction

Man faces a crisis in his relation to the earth. He has been poisoning its rivers, contaminating its soil, polluting its air. Among the historical roots of the exploitative attitudes of Western civilization that have led to the desecration of the environment are an inadequate theology of nature and an obsolete ethic of nature. The central goal of this volume is the articulation of an ecological theology and an ecological ethic.

"The pollution and destruction of man's environment are religious and ethical problems that derive basically from irreverent and immoral attitudes toward nature, rather than from technological inadequacy alone," Harold Schilling writes in Chapter 7. "The solution is not beyond the capabilities of technology—provided it allows itself to be guided by more sensitive religious views and ethical motivations with respect to nature than now prevail generally in our culture." Ecological devastation will simply take new forms unless there are fundamental changes in values and in social institutions. New priorities and new decision-making mechanisms are required for the redirection of technology.

Most of us who have written for this volume would reject two views for which there are many spokesmen today. On the one hand, we take issue with those who advocate purely technical solutions without fundamental changes in values or institutions. We disagree with the "techno-

1

logical optimists" who are confident that if man invented the machine, his ingenuity will also correct any defects in its operation. On the other hand, we differ from those who despair of any significant internal changes in a social and economic order that exploits both man and nature. Such radical critics have in the past often advocated revolutionary action to bring about a redistribution of power. More recently, especially among youth, there have been efforts to develop alternative life styles—such as communes in place of traditional family units—which sometimes express a strongly anti-technological outlook. Despite their ecological awareness and sensitivity to human relationships, these new movements would, if taken as a universal pattern, neglect the positive potential of a technology redirected to genuine human needs and the preservation of the earth.

A number of sources of new attitudes toward nature are explored in these chapters. There are, first, neglected biblical themes, such as man's responsible stewardship and the intrinsic value of all creatures. Then there are crucial ideas deriving from science: nature as a dynamic process, the interdependence of living things, man as part of nature. In addition, there are significant resources in process philosophy, contemporary theology, and oriental traditions. From these various strands, a coherent doctrine of man is formulated—stressing man's unity with nature rather than his separation from it, his existence as an embodied self rather than as a body-soul dualism. The theme of divine immanence in nature is also developed.

An ecological ethic requires not only new attitudes toward the earth but a new analysis of the social context of man's relation to nature and of the political decisions that bear on the uses of technology. Poverty and pollution are linked as products of our economic and industrial institutions. Thus the prophetic demand for social justice is as relevant to environmental deterioration as to urban blight. Four specific problems are analyzed here: control of pollution, restraint in consumption, redirection of technology, and limitation of population.

This book has its origin in a group of scientists, philosophers, and theologians which since 1961 has met for a weekend of discussion twice a year.[1] Many of the earlier papers prepared for these conversations have

---

[1]In addition to the participants in this volume, the group has at various times included: George Bradley (Physics, Western Michigan University), Herman Carr (Physics, Rutgers University), John Dillenberger (Graduate Theological Union, Berkeley), Langdon Gilkey (Divinity School, University of Chicago), Harmon Holcomb (Philosophy, University of Rochester), Claiborne Jones (Zoology, University of North Carolina), John Ollom (Physics, Drew University), Francis O. Schmitt (Neurosciences, M.I.T.), Henry Torrey (Physics, Rutgers University), Charles West (Princeton Theological Seminary). For grants covering travel expenses to these meetings we are indebted to the Danforth Foundation and the Church Society for College Work.

been published elsewhere.[2] The essays from more recent years were revised by their respective authors in the light of the comments and criticisms of the other participants. In a real sense the book is a product of the whole group. It is appropriate that it should be dedicated to Harold Schilling, who was the moving spirit in convening us—though this is not a formal *Festschrift*, and he would undoubtedly protest: *fest* me no *Schrifts*.

In this introductory chapter, I will set forth the main themes of the volume grouped under three headings: (I) Philosophy and Science: Man's Understanding of Nature; (II) Theology and Ecology: Man's Attitudes Toward Nature; (III) Ethics and Technology: Man's Control of Nature.

I. PHILOSOPHY AND SCIENCE: MAN'S UNDERSTANDING OF NATURE

Several basic questions concerning methods of knowing are raised in the opening chapters. First, is the formulation of a theology of nature a legitimate undertaking that can be defended on methodological grounds? Second, in a world of scientific law, how can one speak of divine immanence in nature, an idea that has usually fostered respect for the earth? Third, is our exploitative outlook in part a result of the prevailing Western view of knowledge as objective, rational control? These initial questions may seem somewhat abstract, but they are important if we are to understand the dominant presuppositions of our culture and the possibility of moving beyond them.

In Chapter 2, Frederick Ferré lays a valuable philosophical foundation for subsequent chapters by comparing the methods of science and theology. He starts by criticizing the claim of empiricist philosophers that to explain an event is to show that it is an instance of a scientific law. He

[2]Discussed at early meetings were: William G. Pollard, *Chance and Providence* (New York: Charles Scribner's Sons, 1958) and Langdon Gilkey, *Maker of Heaven and Earth* (Garden City, N.Y.: Doubleday & Company, Inc., 1959). Mimeographed papers presented at subsequent meetings have appeared, with various degrees of revision, in Harold K. Schilling, *Science and Religion* (New York: Charles Scribner's Sons, 1962); Ian G. Barbour, *Issues in Science and Religion* (Englewood Cliffs, N.J.: Prentice-Hall, Inc., 1966); Daniel D. Williams, "How Does God Act? An Essay in Whitehead's Metaphysics" in W. L. Reese and E. Freeman, eds., *Process and Divinity* (LaSalle, Ill.: Open Court Publishing Co., 1964); Huston Smith, "The Death and Rebirth of Metaphysics," ibid.; Langdon Gilkey, "The Concept of Providence in Contemporary Theology," *Journal of Religion*, 43 (1963), 171; Claiborne Jones, "In the Midst of Life," *Church Review*, December 1964; John Compton, "Natural Science and the Experience of Nature," *Journal of Existentialism*, 6 (1966), 203.

defends the explanatory power of theories and models and discusses the role of scientific paradigms that are not directly testable. He argues that understanding rather than prediction and control is the goal of science—an emphasis that itself might encourage greater respect for nature.

Ferré goes on to consider the distinctive types of explanation, of successively wider scope, that are provided by laws, theories, paradigms, and "metaphysical explanations." He sees metaphysics as an extension of the search for coherence; it involves the construction of inclusive conceptual syntheses that will be relevant to aesthetic, moral, and religious as well as scientific experience. But the functions of "ultimate explanations," he suggests, are more valuational than theoretical. They arise from the need for acceptance of the world and for action in it. He concludes that "theological explanation" in terms of personal purpose may indeed lead to an inclusive conceptual synthesis—an extension of the cognitive quest exemplified in science—but it is primarily the fulfillment of a valuational quest that is quite different from science. This conclusion would lead one to give prominence to the attitudinal components of a theology of nature.

Ferré's position reflects the influence of linguistic analysis, the dominant school among contemporary philosophers, which recognizes that differing types of language serve very diverse functions. Religious language is used in a variety of ways. It may recommend a way of life and endorse a set of moral principles. It may propose a distinctive self-understanding and engender characteristic attitudes toward the world. It may direct attention to particular patterns in events, and it may specify a perspective on the world and an interpretation of history and human experience. Religious language has a variety of functions, most of which are rather unlike those of scientific language.[3]

Chapter 3 by John Compton asks how events that can be described by scientific laws can also be thought of as God's action. Drawing from recent work in linguistic philosophy, he proposes an analogy in the way human actions can be described by two very different kinds of language. An arm motion can be analyzed physiologically as a succession of causally linked events, but it can also be analyzed as an action in terms of purpose and intent. A particular action (mailing a letter, for instance) may be performed with an infinite variety of specific bodily movements, but it is not defined by any of them. Yet the agent is not a separate entity acting causally *on* the body; the agent *is* precisely the embodied self in action. There are not two entities, but rather one set of events described in two ways: by causal analysis when considered as bodily movement, and by intentional analysis when considered as purposive action.

[3]See Frederick Ferré, *Language, Logic and God* (New York: Harper & Row, Publishers, 1961).

Compton wants us to conceive of God's action in nature in an analogous fashion. God acts in and through natural events, not by interfering causally from outside. This scientific account describes the causal links among events; yet the same events can be understood as an expression of divine purpose. Nature and history *are* God's action, in this view. This implies a rejection of any radical dualism between God and the world, analogous to the rejection of the mind-body dualism in man. We have two languages for describing a common set of events, a scientific and a theological account of nature. The possibility of representing divine immanence in new ways can in turn engender new attitudes toward nature.

Huston Smith in Chapter 5 shows that the Western identification of knowledge with objective, rational control has contributed to man's separation from nature. He maintains that Western thought since Descartes has emphasized analysis, conceptualization, generalization, and control. The detached observer is separated from an objectified, external world. Nature is an alien and mechanical object to be mastered and conquered by scientific man. Truth is an impersonal set of ideas from which all subjectivity has been eliminated. Professor Smith indicates how each of these assumptions can be challenged from the standpoint of Eastern thought. Here also theories of knowledge and questions of method are seen to have ecological implications.

II. THEOLOGY AND ECOLOGY:
MAN'S ATTITUDES TOWARD NATURE

Theology is systematic and critical reflection by a religious community concerning its beliefs and values. Along with worship and action, it is an expression of the corporate life of a community that has arisen in response to particular historical events; in the religious traditions of the West, the formative events are those of the biblical period. Theology also interprets the ongoing religious and moral experience of the individual and the community. It is a set of human symbols, reflecting changing categories of thought, through which these crucial areas of experience are understood. But these symbols are also used to interpret and evaluate other areas of experience, including man's encounter with the nonhuman world.

Any attempt at a coherent intellectual synthesis must take into account all aspects of experience: religious, moral, aesthetic, and scientific. A theology of nature, in particular, cannot ignore the findings of contemporary science concerning the character of nature. The task, then, is interdisciplinary. An ecological theology will have diverse sources: biblical, scientific, and philosophical. Let us look at each of these in turn.

Biblical sources might at first seem rather unpromising. They have, in fact, been strongly criticized in Lynn White's influential article, "The Historical Roots of Our Ecologic Crisis."[4] White holds that the idea of man's dominion over nature was a major factor in the emergence of the exploitative attitudes typical of Western man. In the opening chapter of Genesis, man is told to "fill the earth and subdue it, and have dominion over the fish of the sea and over the birds of the air and over every living thing." White says that such passages, contrasting man and nature, have led to our attitudes of superiority and arrogance in subjugating the natural world.

Later in the present volume it is argued that White's thesis over-simplifies an extremely complex historical phenomenon. Thus Roger Shinn sees many causative factors in the rise of science and industrial technology, and he also points to the diversity of strands within the Christian tradition, including some that were hostile to science. My own concluding essay suggests that in the biblical record itself there are neglected themes that can provide some of the needed correctives. Biblical man does not claim unlimited dominion; he is trustee and steward, responsible to God in his care of the creation. Moreover, nature is held to have intrinsic value and rights of its own and is not simply an instrument for human purposes; it is a delight to God, quite apart from man. God is concerned for all living things, from the great hippopotamus to the sparrow that falls. Many of the psalms express appreciation, wonder, and humility in response to natural phenomena. And nature is said to participate in the drama of redemption; it will share in the ultimate harmony that is its final fulfillment. We will trace some of these themes in the life of St. Francis, for whom all the creatures were brothers under God.

An equally important biblical resource is the prophetic concern for social justice. The Old Testament reiterates a sense of corporate responsibility for national evils and a passionate attack on inequality and oppression in the social order. Daniel Williams' perceptive essay in Chapter 4 reminds us that in the prophetic tradition "nature and man are bound together in a fateful history where the responsibility of man for his life and for his world meets the demands of a new order in which basic justice is required." This leads Williams to talk about "the politicizing of man's relation to nature." Again, in the New Testament, love is response to the neighbor in need. Today we realize—as first-century man could not—how dependent is the neighbor's welfare upon the environment that surrounds him and upon the impact of technology on that environment. Finally, there is the recurrent vision of a new earth, a Kingdom of justice and

[4]Lynn White, Jr., in *Science*, 155 (1967), 1203.

brotherhood as well as harmony with nature, which serves as a standard of judgment upon the present order.

Yet we must acknowledge that many of these biblical themes have not been strongly represented in recent religious thought. The history of redemption has been the theologian's preoccupation, and the realm of nature and man's relation to it have too often been ignored. In neo-orthodoxy, nature was usually treated as the setting for human redemption. In existentialism, nature was the impersonal stage for the drama of personal existence. In both movements, man was still separated from the natural order, and history was contrasted with nature. Only in the last decade have there been signs of a recovery of more biblical views of nature.[5]

Turning to the second source of a theology of nature, we might list some relevant concepts deriving from contemporary science:

1. *Nature as dynamic process.* From Newton to the nineteenth century, the world was thought of as a machine, static in form and mechanically determined in behavior. Today, nature is known to be an evolving, changing, creative process. There is indeterminacy at the physical level and chance at the level of biological evolution. This is an incomplete cosmos, still coming into being, open to the future. Daniel Williams' chapter emphasizes this concept of "possibility," as well as man's new power over the future. He says that for man, nature is not a fixed setting that must be simply accepted; but neither is it just an object to be manipulated, for it has its own potentialities and limits. Against all forms of determinism—scientific, sociological, or theological—most of the contributors to this volume assert that there are genuine alternatives open—for nature, for man, and even for God.

2. *The interdependence of living things.* Nature is an interacting community. To adopt a "holistic view" (in Schilling's terminology) is to deal with nature as an integrated ecosystem. Ecology is the study of the relations of organisms and environments in the subtly balanced networks that form the web of life. We are more aware today of the marvelous reciprocities and mutualities among creatures, the long food chains linking diverse species, the complex cycles of elements and compounds, the delicate balances that are easily upset. Life-support systems and environments are themselves largely the product of living things. Interdependence, diversity, vulnerability—these are key features of the natural world.

3. *Man's unity with nature.* Man is kin to all creatures, sharing a

---

[5]For example, Joseph Sittler, "Called to Unity," *Ecumenical Review*, Vol. 14 (January 1962). For other examples, see footnotes to Chap. 9.

long evolutionary history and participating in the same creative process. He is part of the interwoven fabric of life. He is quite literally dependent on plants that give out the oxygen he breathes, and on bacteria that purify the water he drinks. As Schilling points out, human qualities of mind and spirit have remarkable parallels in higher animals. A contemporary doctrine of man must represent his historical continuity with other forms of life, as well as his distinctive capacities for language, reflective thought, and culture. Man, in short, is both a biological organism and a responsible self, and he is always part of a larger community. Several authors in this collection reject the classical dualism of body and soul and urge a concept of man as a psychosomatic unity—a person-in-community—a view that is at once more biblical and more contemporary.

4. *The uniqueness of the earth.* The long and extraordinary history of our planet provides the basis for a profound ecological concern in William Pollard's essay (Chapter 6). He delineates the uniqueness of the earth among the barren planets; he shows the narrow limits of gravity, heat, atmosphere, and other conditions for life. He traces the accelerating stages of life—from multicellular organisms 600 million years ago, through the advent of *Homo sapiens* 40,000 years ago, and the industrial revolution 200 years ago, down to the technological affluence in our own lifetime. He holds before us the view of the earth from space, a precious gem of breathtaking beauty. And now man threatens this precarious planet, polluting its air and water, exhausting its rich resources. In this context, it is an act of sacrilege to destroy so rare a gem, to squander the immense creative investment that has gone into its life, to exterminate in a few moments species whose formation took millions of years. Pollard gives a powerful plea to respect the beauty and holiness of the earth, "to celebrate the wonder of the achievement already realized, and to have a holy fear of desecrating her."

I have mentioned some biblical and scientific sources for an ecological theology. A third type of resource is contemporary philosophy. Several of these essays (especially those of Williams, Schilling, and Barbour) reflect the influence of the process philosophy of Alfred North Whitehead. Process thought has incorporated within a systematic metaphysics a number of the themes outlined above: reality as dynamic process, the openness of the future, the interdependence of all events, the rejection of body-mind dualism, and the essential continuity of man with other creatures. Whitehead and his followers picture the world as a community of interacting organisms, characterized by temporality, novelty, and creativity.[6]

Process philosophy has also provided new categories for thinking

---

[6]Alfred North Whitehead, *Science and the Modern World* (New York: The Macmillan Company, 1925); and John B. Cobb, *A Christian Natural Theology* (Philadelphia: The Westminster Press, 1965).

about God's relation to nature. If there is genuine freedom and novelty, even God cannot know the future; there are alternatives that remain open until actions are taken by individual agents. According to this view, God influences the world but respects its integrity. He shares with the world the responsibility for the future. Here is a model of divine power as love, persuasion, and evocation of response, rather than as omnipotent coercion or predetermination. God does not act directly, but participates in the unfolding of every event. He acts with and through other causes; he is the source of both order and novelty. Every entity must respond for itself, and nothing that happens is God's doing alone.

The new theism of process thought recovers the idea of divine immanence. Instead of a God who intervenes from outside, there is creativity present throughout cosmic history. This representation avoids setting either God or man in sharp opposition to nature. Such a view not only recognizes man's dependence on the natural order but encourages respect for all forms of life. It leads to a respect for life that would nurture an ecological conscience.

We should also note more personal and immediate kinds of response to immanence in nature. Several contributors refer to Loren Eiseley's writings,[7] which express a response of awe and wonder and a sense of the numinous, a sensitivity to beauty and mystery that is crowded out by the technological mentality of manipulation and control. But in Schilling's essay such sensitivity is eloquently manifest, together with more rational arguments from scientific ecology. Schilling calls for a "holistic ethic" whose criterion is the conservation and enhancement of wholeness and communality. He concludes that the twofold biblical commandment (love of God and neighbor) should now be threefold, embracing also a love of nature.

In addition to these currents in Western thought, there are traditions in the East from which we can learn much concerning attitudes toward the natural world. Huston Smith's essay describes the organic unity of self, society, and nature in the religions of India and China. He gives vivid examples of the sense of harmony with nature expressed in Taoism, and elaborates ideas of the interpenetration and interdependence of all things and of the hidden unity of the apparently opposed (the yang-yin principle). He acknowledges that whereas the West tends toward aggressive activism, Eastern religions run the risk of passive quietism and acceptance of the social injustices of the status quo. But he suggests that the Eastern approach does have ethical as well as ecological implications, and that the values of surrender, harmony, and simplicity have been sadly neglected in the West.

[7]Loren Eiseley, *The Immense Journey* (New York: Random House, Inc., 1957).

III.   ETHICS AND TECHNOLOGY:
MAN'S CONTROL OF NATURE

We must look finally at the social context of man's relation to nature and at the political decisions whereby technology and pollution can be controlled. Ecological devastation calls for communal responsibility and not simply individual conscience. Responsibility, I take it, requires examining in advance the consequences of any action for all beings affected by it and acting with sensitivity to their needs. Since environmental effects are usually regional or global rather than local, many of the crucial policy decisions must be made by large communities of men, and hence politically.

Earth Day was opposed by some of the social activists because they viewed it as a diversion from the problems of the ghetto and poverty. I would reply that pollution and urban blight reflect a common set of cultural values and a common set of economic institutions. The exploitation of nature and that of man are two sides of the same coin. Conversely, the transformation of exploitative attitudes and institutions will enrich both human and nonhuman life. Uncontrolled technology, in particular, is the major source of both pollution and economic inequality. It has increased the gap between rich and poor nations, and between the cultures of affluence and poverty in our own nation. The dispossessed have received proportionately less of its benefits and more of its harmful effects.

The prophetic passion for social justice is just as important as respect for nature, in encouraging an ecological conscience. The issue of justice is present in all ecological problems, seen now in the complexity of their interrelationships. There are conflicting interests among nations and social groups, in addition to the rights and needs of lower forms of life. Taxation, antipollution legislation, and control of the environment and of natural resources are matters of public policy. Moreover the processes of decision making and the structures of political power themselves need alteration if technology is to become an instrument of justice.

A new interest in these social and ethical issues is evident among scientists. As Roger Shinn indicates in his essay, it is no longer assumed that science will automatically advance human welfare. To be sure, some scientists (particularly in "fundamental research") still disavow all responsibility for the uses to which their discoveries may be put. Others (particularly in "applied science") hold that a scientific elite should be given power to make and carry out social planning, since rational decision making requires technical knowledge. Shinn defends a third alternative:

The scientist, both as citizen and as technical adviser, should participate in the wider governmental processes through which priorities and policies are established. Once again, the context of social ethics is inescapably political.

Among the specific problems in ethics and technology discussed in this volume, four receive more extended treatment:

1. Control of pollution. We need a variety of special laws providing enforceable national standards for auto emissions, air and water effluents from cities and industries, long-lasting pesticides and detergents, radiation and thermal pollution, solid waste disposal, and the like. But beyond such attacks on specific hazards, we must make sure that the social costs of any technological product are included in its price. New methods of social accounting and of taxes and incentives must allow the cost of preserving the environment and of disposing of all wastes from a product to be assessed against its manufacturer. On the positive side, the creation of new technologies that are ecologically sound—especially in transportation, in the chemical industries, and in the recycling of materials—should be an urgent national goal.

2. Restraint in consumption. Our appetites as consumers are stimulated by a barrage of advertising. The frantic pursuit of affluence and comfort leads to scandalous waste and the rapid exhaustion of resources. Power consumption is doubling every eight or ten years. In place of the dream of an ever-expanding gross national product, we must begin to look to a steady-state economy in most fields, with growth occurring only in service occupations and in technological improvements (as judged by ecological and human standards rather than by efficiency and productivity alone). The motive is not an ascetic world-denial or a romantic return to the primitive, but a deliberate determination to live within the earth's finite resources and carrying capacity.

3. Redirection of technology. The profits of the marketplace are an inadequate mechanism for the control of technological innovation. New decision-making procedures for technology assessment within the federal government are proposed, in which social consequences are thoroughly studied in advance; those groups most likely to be affected should be represented at the early stages of innovation before vested interests are strongly entrenched. In our national priorities, the abolition of hunger, poverty, and pollution at home and abroad should come before luxury goods. We have invested heavily in aerospace and military technology, but not in public transportation, urban housing, or pollution abatement.

Only by deliberate policy can technology become an instrument to reduce, rather than increase, the gap between rich and poor.

   4. Limitation of population. In underdeveloped countries, famine and social chaos produced by overpopulation are imminent threats of disaster. But in technologically advanced countries also, measures against pollution and poverty will be ineffective unless the population explosion is halted. The United States, with 6 percent of the world's population, uses up natural resources as fast as all the rest of the world put together. One American baby will in his lifetime consume roughly 50 times as much raw material as a baby born in India. It is already evident that to check population growth, voluntary family planning is not enough. Intensive education promoting the idea of smaller families, and the development of social and economic incentives and penalties, as well as research on inexpensive, long-lasting contraceptive pills, must receive massive funding in a major national and worldwide program to limit population growth.

   The image of earth as a spaceship has come to symbolize the interdependence and finitude of our globe. Resources and environment are limited, materials must be recycled and not recklessly squandered. But Harold Schilling suggests that the spaceship image, taken alone, may be too static. Man's role is not only to preserve, but to develop and improve. The aim is not simply to "maintain the balance" or to "avoid interfering with nature," but to transform the earth responsibly. The world is incomplete; it has creative possibilities, including further evolutionary development, in which man can have a hand. Schilling proposes that along with the spaceship symbol we need the biblical symbol of the garden and the gardener—with man as the steward under God. But, he adds, man is now known to be part of the garden and not separate from it. If responsibility and interdependence are recognized, man's new powers over nature need not be disavowed; they can be exercised sensitively and creatively rather than destructively.

   As they look to the future, these authors acknowledge the possibility of catastrophe, but they also see hopeful signs. Pollard says that crucial times of judgment in the past have often been preludes to creative advances. He believes we are on the threshold of a new postcivilization in which most of our existing institutions will be left behind. The nation-state is obsolete; only a new global civilization, a world order under law, can deal with problems that are international in scope. Man indeed has amazing new powers to control disease, to abolish poverty and hunger, to establish worldwide communications, to create in the laboratory new materials and new forms of life. We have before us the vision of a new earth, a global garden at one with its gardener. Clifford Bax's hymn, which opened this book, closes with an affirmation: "Earth shall be fair, and all her people one."

IAN G. BARBOUR is Professor of Religion and Professor of Physics at Carleton College. He was formerly chairman of the Physics Department at Kalamazoo College. His published works include Christianity and the Scientist, Issues in Science and Religion, Science and Secularity: The Ethics of Technology, *and, as editor,* Science and Religion: New Perspectives on the Dialogue. *Articles of his have appeared in scientific, philosophical, religious, and educational journals.*

FREDERICK FERRÉ

2

Explanation
In Science
and Theology

Is the idea of a theology of nature intelligible in an age of science?
Is the formulation of an ecological theology a legitimate undertaking that
can be defended on methodological grounds? Might theology have something significant to say about nature—or is nature the exclusive domain of
science? We must try to answer these basic questions about the justification of the theological enterprise itself before we can attempt in subsequent chapters to formulate specific details of a theology of nature.

My aim in this chapter is to consider what we are trying to do when
we seek to understand our world as scientists, philosophers, theologians
—and, more importantly, as whole men concerned about the whole earth.
Ecological awareness has taught us, among other things, that there are
too many compartments in our society and in our thought. We must think,
and think wisely, if we are to find an adequate philosophy for living
together on this small planet.

This chapter will aim, therefore, at clarifying what I believe to be
the proper relationship between the kinds of thinking done by scientists,
philosophers, and theologians. It will do this by analyzing various kinds
of "explanation." The chapter will also challenge the common assumption
that explanation and evaluation must always be kept in compartments
sealed from each other. An epistemology suited for an ecologically
conscious age must learn how to relate not merely different facts, not

merely different modes of explanation, but different essential aspects of our own human consciousness itself. Only when we come to terms with the attitudinal component always effective in our fundamental modes of thinking about the universe will we be able to recognize and utilize the very human logic of ultimate explanations.

To the reader unfamiliar with the discussion among philosophers of science in recent years, the first part of this argument may seem uncomfortably dry. I ask such readers, however, to bear with the next few pages. Scientific explanations are the key to our culture's understanding of explanation itself; thus without seeing how the interests of science themselves create a deeper thirst than some philosophers have been willing to recognize, we would miss seeing the essential human continuities between proximate or limited explanations and the larger explanatory forms toward which we are fumbling—with such urgent need—today.

One of the more nerve-shattering challenges to theology from science —or what has been widely supposed to be from science—has been the raising of grave doubts about the logical possibility, or the intellectual propriety, of dealing in what I shall call "ultimate explanations." This challenge arises from a view of scientific method rather than from any substantive discoveries made by the sciences. It is therefore better thought of as a challenge coming from scientists and philosophers reflecting on scientific procedures, rather than from science directly; but this challenge is none the less a serious inhibition to one of the traditional roles of religious thinking, particularly in regard to a theology of nature, as long as it is able plausibly to claim the authority and prestige of first-order scientific practice to support it.

I. EXPLANATION AS DEDUCTION
FROM SCIENTIFIC LAWS

The attack consists in two claims, both of which I intend to dispute. The first claim is that an explanation *within science* is always analyzable into a deductive pattern in which the statement of what is to be explained is derivable as a conclusion from a set of premises, premises usually containing particular statements of initial conditions and always containing the statement of at least one general law. According to this view, "subsumption under a law" is crucial for every scientific explanation. In agreement with widespread usage, therefore, I shall call this first claim the "covering law" view of scientific explanation: a scientific explanation is provided if and only if the event or law to be explained is brought under, or "covered" by, a law expressing a general regularity of nature. For example; the bursting of one's frozen water pipes might be explained in this manner by reference to the universal proposition that *all* water expands upon freezing.

The second claim is that scientific explanations, as conceived by the covering law view, are *the only genuine explanations*. Anything else is, at best, only an "incomplete explanation" in which whatever is put forward as explanatory—whether it be similarities with already familiar domains, "understood" personal motivations, or the like—will have "explanatory value only if it involves at least tacit reference to general laws."[1] Mere familiarity, for instance, may give us a comfortable feeling or a sense of being at home with the subject matter, but according to the covering law view, this is both potentially misleading[2] and logically irrelevant ("the extent to which an idea will be considered as familiar varies from person to person and from time to time, and a psychological factor of this kind certainly cannot serve as a standard in assessing the worth of a proposed explanation"[3]). Likewise, a sense of understanding motives may give emphatic vividness to an explanation of personal behavior, but this is cognitively unreliable and really nothing more than a special case of the appeal to familiarity, familiarity that comes from our own experience of purposive behavior.[4]

It is claimed, in short, that *every* sound explanation must subsume the event to be explained under general laws.[5] Since theological thinking is not engaged in the enterprise of formulating general laws of nature, it must be supposed that any explanation offered by theology will be methodologically unsound.

Now it is not my heroic—but absurd—intention to deny that many theological explanations of the total scheme of things have been unsound, since I suspect that a great many such candidates for ultimate explanation have been egregiously faulty, for a variety of reasons. But I believe that the wholesale disposal of them is at least equally unsound, and that the dismissal of all efforts at constructing ultimate explanations (culminating, as I shall argue, in religious forms of ultimate explanation) does injustice to the flexibility and power of human thought on several fronts, the scientific as well as the metaphysical and theological.

Let us start by looking at the sciences themselves. The covering law view has serious defects as a "reconstructed logic of scientific method,"[6]

---

[1]Carl G. Hempel and Paul Oppenheim, "Studies in the Logic of Explanation," reprinted in Edward H. Madden, ed., *The Structure of Scientific Thought* (Boston: Houghton Mifflin Company, 1960), p. 22.
[2]Ibid., p. 28.
[3]Ibid., p. 29.
[4]Ibid., p. 29.
[5]Ibid., p. 29, italics added.
[6]See Abraham Kaplan, *The Conduct of Inquiry* (San Francisco: Chandler Publishing Co., 1964), especially Chap. 1.

and these have been the subject of an extensive literature in the past decade. I shall not attempt even to summarize recent debate, but for our purposes three areas of weakness are particularly pertinent. First, it is doubtful whether one can long maintain that *only* when a covering law is known can we claim to possess a genuine explanation. We may, I think, agree that *often* the deductive scheme portrayed by the covering law view is present in scientific explanation, particularly in such fields as physics or astronomy. We may even admire the precision and rigor of such deductive explanations and begin to wish that all explanations could be similarly patterned. But it becomes costly to insist that unless our explanations in science conform to these few fortunate ones, they are not really scientific explanations at all. In light of the actual situation within recognized and responsible scientific enterprises, it becomes increasingly evident that such tenacious holding to the covering law view slips quietly into techniques of persuasive definition for "explanation."

What is the actual situation? The simple but unavoidable answer is that a great many of our explanations in science cannot provide laws of the sort deemed necessary by the covering law view. The explanatory power, for example, of the concept of evolution—including even the so-called law of natural selection—does not function in the way we would expect if only subsumption under a specific natural regularity qualified for scientific explanation. These principles do not permit deductive prediction of the specific course of the history of biological forms, though they do greatly aid our understanding of it. Even more obviously, social and psychological sciences must function without recourse to such covering laws from which (taken together with statements of initial conditions) the phenomena could be uniquely deduced. Laws permitting us to deduce the outbreak of civil war in a society, or the falling in love of a particular couple, are not even a realistic hope on the horizon. Even an author who has defended the covering law view acknowledges that in the sciences of human behavior we simply lack covering laws that will fulfill the supposed requirement, and (he adds significantly) "it is worthy of note that we do not deny ourselves the claim that we have explained . . . because of this."[7]

It appears, then, that there is a wider but still legitimate and needed use of the concept "explanation," even within science, that is not included in the covering law view. Subsumption under a law may indeed form an important kind of scientific explanation, but it turns out not to be a necessary condition for all such explanation. The weakness of the covering law view is hidden, for a time, behind the vague assertion that the general laws need only be implicit. But where it becomes evident that there simply

[7]John Hospers, "What Is Explanation?" in Antony Flew, ed., *Essays in Conceptual Analysis* (New York: The Macmillan Company, 1956), p. 105.

are no known laws of the sort called for in the appeal to "at least tacit reference to general laws,"[8] the case either fails or is driven to the high but barren ground of a priori assertion and persuasive definition.

Second, even the presence of general regularities of nature may not, by itself, be sufficient to provide a complete scientific explanation. That an event can be shown deductively to be an instance of a more general pattern of events observed in nature very often will not satisfy a scientist that it has been explained. Why is *that* pattern found and not some other? What is it that *accounts* for this general regularity? Sometimes, perhaps, the answers will be sought, as the covering law view holds, in subsuming the law in question under some still more general law, deducing the regularity from other wider regularities, just as one might attempt the "derivation of the general regularities governing the motion of double stars from the laws of celestial mechanics. . . ."[9] But sometimes even this will not be enough to answer the scientist's quest for explanation. He wants to have some idea of the structures, the underlying mechanisms, by reference to which the regularities he observes may become intelligible rather than merely arbitrary. All the laws in his possession, together with a full grasp of their deductive relationships, may not add up to a single explanation in this fuller sense of the word. On the contrary, the natural regularities themselves, even the widest he can observe, may become the problematic phenomena crying out for explanation rather than supplying it. The covering law view thus fails in its account of the scientific enterprise, since it may be possible to have laws in abundance but still not to have an explanation.

II. THE EXPLANATORY POWER
OF THEORIES

This consideration brings us, then, to the third and most revealing defect in the covering law claim I am criticizing. This defect is the failure to make adequate provision for scientific *theory* in the "reconstructed logic" of science. It would be dangerously misleading, as much current discussion has shown, to make the distinction too sharp between the laws and the theories of a science. What we observe is deeply influenced by what theoretical language we employ, just as our theories are scientifically useful to the extent that they remain in fruitful touch with observation. But be this as it may, there is in the covering law view a strange neglect of the differences between what constitutes the statement of an observed

[8]Hempel and Oppenheim, "Logic of Explanation," p. 22.
[9]Ibid., p. 21.

regularity of nature and what constitutes the statement of an inferred "regularity" of a theoretical entity or structure. This neglect is illustrated in the following passage:

> To an observer in a row boat, that part of an oar which is under water appears to be bent upwards. The phenomenon is explained by means of general laws—namely the law of refraction and the law that water is an optically denser medium than air—and by reference to certain antecedent conditions—especially the fact that part of the oar is in the water, part in the air, and that the oar is practically a straight piece of wood. . . . But the question "Why?" may be raised also in regard to general laws. Thus . . . the question might be asked: Why does the propagation of light conform to the law of refraction? Classical physics answers in terms of the undulatory theory of light, i.e. by stating that the propagation of light is a wave phenomenon of a certain general type, and that all wave phenomena of that type satisfy the law of refraction. Thus, the explanation of a general regularity consists in subsuming it under another, more comprehensive regularity, under a more general law.[10]

What is evident here is the running together of two quite different types of laws. The first is a law that we may say, roughly, is a law of gross observation. We see oars as bent regularly under certain circumstances. We see refraction effects of other sorts, inside and outside the laboratory. But neither in nor out of our laboratories do we *see* light waves being propagated like water waves in a pond. We can, indeed, observe regularities of various sorts—interference patterns and the like—that are highly encouraging to our theories that light can sometimes be represented as being in certain ways like "wave phenomena of a certain type." The point is, however, that in moving from explanation by subsumption under *observable* natural regularities (what Comte called positive general facts[11]) to explanation by reference to *supposed* regularities of structure (which make sense out of the given observable regularities of nature), the step has been taken to a logically very different type of explanation. The crucial importance of this step is obscured by the covering law view.

There is a practical consequence, too, embedded in this logical distinction. There is a difference between, on the one hand, treating nature as a black box whose behavior we note, generalize upon, and predict with considerable effectiveness, and, on the other hand, approaching the world with additional interests in understanding what may be behind the visible structures and behaviors. If we ignore this distinction, we may be lured uncritically into the false belief that the discovery of uniform correlations

---

[10]Ibid., p. 20.
[11]See August Comte, *Introduction to Positive Philosophy*, ed. Frederick Ferré (Indianapolis: The Bobbs-Merrill Co., Inc., 1969).

between events is the most important part of our cognitive endeavors. And this may, as a practical consequence, lead us to focus attention too fixedly on the quest for uniformities and still more uniformities in nature—to the neglect of the search for theories and models through which alone these uniformities can be made intelligible to us.

The methodological point here at issue is the difference between what Margenau calls the *correlational* and the *theoretic* procedures within science,[12] or what Toulmin more vividly, and with perhaps more glee, contrasts as "natural history" (or "mere bug-hunting"[13]) versus "physics."[14] The former is interested in finding "regularities of given forms," whereas the latter is in quest of "the form of given regularities."[15] This distinction —of the greatest importance however it may be phrased—is ignored and indeed denied by any proposal that "to explain an event is simply to bring it under a law; and to explain a law is to bring it under another law."[16] Such an account would send us hunting on the surface of our experience for more empirical regularities, whereas actually what may be most needed (even for eventual practical control) are what Margenau terms the "subsurface connections," always most highly acclaimed by working scientists.[17]

Illustrations of the enormous difference of explanatory power exhibited by these "subsurface connections" as contrasted with "uniformities" are not difficult to find. For example, practical knowledge of the relationships holding between the lengths of the sides of the three-four-five right triangle long antedated the Pythagorean theorem; this regularity of form was used for surveying land before the time of Pythagoras as well as after.

> Yet we pay homage to Pythagoras' mathematical demonstration. . . . Why should it be so important to devise a proof which adds nothing to the empirical knowledge already available? What distinguishes the Greek philosopher from the careful observers in Egypt? The answer is: Through his act a *theory* was born; the surface of mere correlation was broken, subsurface explanation had begun.[18]

The usefulness of theory, on the basis of which we may give *reasons* for a particular event happening or for a particular correlation, is further

---

[12]Henry Margenau, *The Nature of Physical Reality* (New York: McGraw-Hill Book Company, 1950), pp. 25–30.
[13]Stephen Toulmin, *The Philosophy of Science* (New York: Harper & Row, Publishers, 1960), p. 54.
[14]Ibid., p. 53.
[15]Ibid.
[16]Hospers, "What Is Explanation?" p. 98.
[17]Margenau, *The Nature of Physical Reality*, p. 29.
[18]Ibid., p. 28.

illustrated by the explanatory advance represented by Bohr's theory-cum-model of the hydrogen atom, an advance that gave *reasons* for the success of Balmer's formula in stating the "uniformity of nature" discovered in the absorption lines of the hydrogen spectrum. "Again, in the proof, a theory of the atom was born. An internal luminosity suddenly shone through the empirical formula."[19]

What is it about a theory-cum-model that provides our higher-level explanations with this "internal luminosity" that is denied to less powerful explanations limited to statements of empirical uniformities? The answer, were it to be fully developed, would center around the *connections in thought* provided by theories, the finding of shared patterns in widely diverse concepts about quite varied phenomena, the fittingness of our ideas together according to the canons of logic, and the discovery of analogues where previously none had been evident—in sum, in the replacement of sheer multiplicity with coherence, the substitution of imaginative acquaintance for opaque strangeness, the elimination or diminution of the sense of the sheerly disconnected and arbitrary.

Perhaps we may have discovered at this point the correct logical place of "familiarity" in explanation. The covering law view was no doubt quite correct in rejecting, as we say, the over-simple appeal to the familiar; such an appeal would, if allowed, short-circuit the entire theoretical enterprise by demanding that explanations be forbidden to venture beyond the already known. But granting the dangers implicit in premature concern for the familiar, we may also recognize the large role which familiarity—of pattern, of operation, of conceptual relation, and the like—plays in the logic of explanation. True, familiarity is a relative notion, but explanations, likewise, must explain to *someone* if they are to function as explanations at all. To this extent, explanation is also a relative notion; but in this sense—in which all language is relative to some user/interpreter —the relativity of both notions becomes decidedly innocuous.

III. EXPLANATORY PARADIGMS IN SCIENCE

The battle for understanding is none other than the war against "unfamiliarity," in its widest sense of incoherence and arbitrariness; science is the human spirit's most carefully constructed and consciously invented instrument for the waging of this war. Thus the internal demands of all the sciences press toward wider and still wider models and theories. The special sciences themselves, as we shall see, cannot remain true to

[19]Ibid., p. 29.

their own particular role in man's cognitive quest and at the same time respond to the drive toward theories and models of *unlimited* comprehensiveness; but the push toward such all-encompassing theories is implicit within the sciences, and therefore the rationally disciplined attempt at forming such schemes of unlimited scope is continuous, though not identical, with the goal of the sciences.

That the special sciences are in search of explanations that would be *basic relative to their own fields of application* has long been recognized by philosophers of science. "*Basic*" here does not need to involve "finality" in the sense of "never-to-be-superseded"; basic explanations are not usefully defined as "incorrigible" ones. Instead, they should be recognized as "final" in the sense that although accepted they themselves do not call for, or admit of, further explanation. That such explanations have in fact been part of the logic of the special sciences, and that these explanatory paradigms have not proved incorrigible, has been reemphasized, among others by Stephen Toulmin and Thomas Kuhn.[20]

Toulmin points out that underlying the lesser explanations of the sciences have always been what he calls "ideals of natural order."[21] It is on the basis of some such ideal that the scientist is content to rest his case. Ideals may vary with the era, but the reliance on them is undeniable; the ideal of natural order represents what the scientist considers to be beyond the need of explanation. For Copernicus, Toulmin shows, this self-explanatory principle was uniform circular motion. "He felt no need to look for interplanetary forces in order to explain why the planets follow closed orbits: in his opinion, a uniform circular motion needed no further explanation, and would—in the nature of things—continue to maintain itself indefinitely."[22] Scientific explanations may seldom in practice be pushed back to these bedrock concepts, but "about any explanatory theory . . . we can always ask what it implies about the Natural Order. There must always be some point in a scientist's explanation where he comes to a stop: beyond this point, if he is pressed to explain further the fundamental basis of his explanation, he can say only that he has reached rock-bottom."[23]

Still, the ideal of natural order that serves the scientist as a basic explanation within his field (e.g., "The natural state of motion is circular") will never—so long as it remains a scientific conception—be a totally inclusive one (e.g., "All events happen as God wills"). The reason for this

[20]Stephen Toulmin, *Foresight and Understanding* (Bloomington: Indiana University Press, 1961), p. 28; Thomas S. Kuhn, *The Structure of Scientific Revolutions* (Chicago: University of Chicago Press, 1962).

[21]Toulmin, *Foresight and Understanding*, p. 41ff.

[22]Ibid., p. 42.

[23]Ibid.

is the fact that the scientist qua scientist has contracted for the task of discovering "why this happened *rather than that*, and the theological explanation will not enable him to make this discrimination. . . ."[24] To protect the very *specificity* of the *special* sciences, it is essential that even their most wide-ranging "ideals of natural order" renounce every pretense at providing a basis for the coherent understanding of *all* things. In a sense, perhaps, this reminder may be no more than a tautology: that the special sciences have specialized jobs to do. But if it is a tautology, it is an important one to keep in mind. And it has practical consequences: e.g., that the physicist qua physicist may properly remain aloof from certain phenomena that the biologist qua biologist finds extremely important, and, in like manner, that a thinker is no longer acting simply qua special scientist when he considers the connections between all that lies within the purview of each of the sciences. Every special science contributes toward our understanding; but no one should too quickly suppose (nor is it any part of the special scientist's job to claim) that all things can be understood in terms of the explanations, even the basic explanatory paradigms, of any such science. It may have made sense to Copernicus, for example, that the only "natural and self-explanatory" notion would be circular; but this had to do with motions and not with "the sum of things entire." For Newton and for ourselves, his descendants, the one form of motion not requiring further explanation (straight-line motion in a vacuum) is of a quite different character. The consequences for physics of the change in these explanatory paradigms are of the highest importance; yet the difference between the Copernican and the Newtonian notion of "rock-bottom" for the explanatory regression remains a difference *within physics*, with clear physical implications and clear conceptual boundaries.

We may here note in passing that although such concepts as these remain part of the explanatory logic of the special sciences, the means of testing them is considerably more elaborate and indirect than is often acknowledged by many popular analyses of scientific procedure. Hospers, for example, insists that every concept used as an explanatory premise in a science must be open to empirical falsification. "Without this condition it would not be considered an explanation in any science."[25] True, but the meaning of falsification—once one admits the role of theories as well as experimental laws, and explanatory paradigms of natural order as well as theories—must be enriched beyond the simplistic look-and-see concept of the "crucial experiment" that has hobbled the philosophy of science—though not the sciences themselves—for far too long.

The means of verification or falsification of these most far-reaching

---

[24]Hospers, "What Is Explanation?" p. 107.
[25]Ibid., p. 108.

concepts or models of the natural order depend upon the scope, the coherence, the consistency, and the practical effectiveness of the entire theoretical structure of the science founded upon them. "Such models and ideals, principles of regularity and explanatory paradigms, are not always recognized for what they are; differences of opinion about them give rise to some of the profoundest scientific disputes, and changes in them to some of the most important changes in scientific theory...."[26] The substitution of Newton's view of straight-line motion as needing "no explanation" in place of Copernicus' satisfaction with the "self-explanatory" character of "natural" circular motion had more to do with the entire schemes of thought of which these models were a basic part than any simple empirical observation. And the adoption of Galileo's fundamental concept of impetus in place of Aristotle's was (despite the "Leaning Tower" myth) more the result of harder cerebration than the result of closer observation.[27]

IV. METAPHYSICAL EXPLANATION
AND THE SEARCH FOR COHERENCE

But, at last, when the most wide-ranging concepts of any science—those to which other explanations keep returning—are "verified" by the cognitive and practical effectiveness of the articulated science, there yet remains an element of the arbitrary and the disconnected. The logical element of disconnection must haunt the basic concepts of every special science, as we have seen, *just as long as these sciences defend their specificity*; and the sense of the arbitrary must cling to every notion that is accepted as rock-bottom, to which one can only shrug and say, "That's just the way it is." Something in all of us dislikes this shrug. That something is what initiated the cognitive quest and initially set the sciences their task: to bring us understanding. Must the quest end here?

Hospers believes that it must, and although he cautions us against prematurely supposing that we have *found* a basic law or a rock-bottom explanation, he points out that if we did actually have a basic law, it would not only be a waste of time but would also be logically self-contradictory to request an explanation of it, since such a move would be "a request for explanation in a situation where by one's own admission no more explain-

[26]Toulmin, *Foresight and Understanding*, pp. 42–43.

[27]Cf. Herbert Butterfield, *The History of Modern Science*, for an account that does not overlook the experimental elements contributing to Aristotle's overthrow but that at the same time makes vivid the *conceptual* revolution underlying the birth of modern science. For further examples, see Toulmin's *Foresight and Understanding*, especially Chaps. 3 and 4.

ing can be done."[28] The demands of theory, that "basic" must mean what it says, would seem to lead inevitably to the frustration of our unquenchable thirst for understanding! Hospers adds:

> Like so many others, this point may seem logically compelling but psychologically unsatisfying. Having heard the above argument, one may still feel inclined to ask, "Why are the basic uniformities of the universe the way they are, and not some other way? Why should we have just *these* laws rather than other ones? I want an *explanation* of why they are as they are." I must confess here, as an autobiographical remark, that I cannot help sharing this feeling: I want to ask why the laws of nature, being contingent, are as they are, even though I cannot conceive of what an explanation of this would be like, and even though by my own argument above the request for such an explanation is self-contradictory.[29]

To account for this psychological dissatisfaction, Hospers blames habit—the mere habit of asking "Why?" even when it makes no sense to do so.

But perhaps the source lies deeper. Our previous analysis of the concept of explanation in terms of the drive to theoretical coherence and completeness may dissuade us, first, from accepting Hospers' identification of the source of our unrest as *merely* psychological. Perhaps there is a built-in drive within the logic of explanation that refuses to be quieted until satisfied; perhaps the human mind properly declines, therefore, to accept the boundaries often proposed for its cognitive aspirations. Perhaps it *must* so decline, for good reasons, despite acknowledgment (with Kant) that the terms of its explanatory paradigms can never be known to be meaningfully applicable in precisely the same ways as are those of its less ambitious theories.

But, second, granting that there are "psychological" sources to our reluctance to abandon the quest for ultimate explanatory satisfaction, the existentialists direct our attention—possibly with some perceptiveness—to a less trivial human basis than "habit." They point to man's anxiety for himself and for his world in the face of (what used to be called) its "contingency," and to his fear of the abyss of meaninglessness that yawns behind the starkly arbitrary. But it is here, poised over this abyss, that the special sciences are entitled—and obliged—to leave us. Whether all men actually feel, or are capable of feeling, or latently feel (deep down), such "ontological anxiety" is not a question that needs to be answered in this paper. It is enough to note that at least some men find their cognitive aspirations reinforced by profound anxieties about what we have learned

[28]Hospers, "What Is Explanation?" p. 116.
[29]Ibid.

to call man's "existential situation." And they discover that even the broadest explanations of the special sciences are unable to answer fully either the cognitive or the personal demand.

Still, the creative energies behind the human struggle against arbitrariness and disconnection have not been exhausted in giving birth to their offspring, the sciences. Prior to the development of the sort of rational inquiry that gave rise to the sciences, of course, conceptual syntheses were frequently attempted—and with sometimes impressive results. But we shall find that adequate ultimate explanations for our own time cannot be divorced from the principles and findings of the scientific method, undoubtedly the most significant intellectual fact of our modern world. How, then, can we proceed responsibly beyond the special sciences in quest of cognitive satisfaction?

First, to overcome "disconnection" by coherence and to provide familiarity of pattern in the place of sheer diversity, theories and models drawn from the special sciences as well as from other sources are quite often used outside the methodological restrictions of scope imposed by their strictly scientific uses. Julian Huxley's or Pierre Teilhard de Chardin's concepts of "evolution," for example, or Alfred North Whitehead's thoughts on "organism"—one could multiply examples—these are in their new contexts given conceptual functions as all-embracing interpretive principles for thought, feeling, and behavior that far transcend the boundaries of their original employment. As a result, these new uses are as vulnerable as fish in a barrel to the accurate fire of those[30] who proceed to demonstrate that these new uses, in attempting to bring coherence to reality as a whole, no longer have the right (*in* this new employment) to claim the authority and precision of the special sciences from which they were borrowed.

These critics are right—of course. This much is built into the very nature of the case. What is not so clear is whether or not such a line of criticism meets the relevant issues: *Must* all explanations have no more than specialized scientific uses? May not concepts be put to work in disciplined ways to bring coherence to our account of reality-as-a-whole as well as to reality-as-delimited-by-our-departments-of-science? The demands for conceptual coherence are surely not prima facie irrelevant to the *whole*, though relevant to the *parts*, of our account of reality.

Some more profound point must lie behind these recent criticisms than the mere platitude that attempting to explain the whole is not the same thing as attempting to explain the part! It may be that underneath such criticisms there still persists the view—residuum of more exciting

---

[30]See Stephen Toulmin, "Scientific Theories and Scientific Myths," in *Metaphysical Beliefs*, ed. A. MacIntyre (London: SCM Press, 1957).

"principles" from positivist days of not so long ago—that "explanations of the whole" *cannot* be put to work in a "disciplined" manner, since "discipline" implies "testing," and "testing" (here lurks the ghost) implies "looking and seeing." But this assumption is false. It must be questioned and questioned again, until the spook is exorcised. Disciplined inquiry does demand tests, but there are conditions under which the tests, on their theoretical side, must be extremely general and, on their experimental side, must be extremely indirect. We have already seen examples of this indirectness and generality of verification in connection with basic explanatory paradigms in the special sciences. We should be prepared for a like situation—intensified—when we turn from models and theories that are taken as "basic relative to a given field" to evaluate models and theories that are offered as ultimate for all knowledge.[31]

Supposing, then, what is at least possible, that our account of things has (to some extent) been unified and given coherence through the disciplined employment of a conceptual synthesis of some kind. We will have overcome (to that extent) the enemy of "disconnection." What, though, of the threat to cognition posed by "arbitrariness"? There are those who maintain that the latter is inescapable and that we shall do well to settle peacefully for the greatest degree of coherence we can find. Alfred North Whitehead puts it: "In a sense, all explanation must end in ultimate arbitrariness. My demand is, that the ultimate arbitrariness of matter of fact from which our formulation starts should disclose the same general principles of reality, which we dimly discern as stretching away into regions beyond our explicit powers of discernment."[32]

V. ULTIMATE EXPLANATION AS VALUATIONAL

Shall we rest content with this verdict? From the viewpoint of pure theory, it is probably the most that can be said, especially if we may also hope, as Whitehead does, that "the sheer statement, of what things are, may contain elements explanatory of why things are."[33] But man's cognitive quest, although carried on in the terms and by the canons of theory, is not for the sake of theory alone. The sense of values and the need for

---

[31] For a more detailed discussion of the appropriate tests that may be applied to models and theories of this latter kind, see the present author's chapters in *Exploring the Logic of Faith*, by Kent Bendall and Frederick Ferré (New York: Association Press, 1962).

[32] *Science and the Modern World* (New York: The Macmillan Company, 1925); Mentor Books edition, p. 88.

[33] Ibid.

action are as much a part of the demand for explanation as the thirst for theory. It may even be the case, indeed, that all theory is for the sake of the life-oriented domain.[34] And if so, then the very concept of cognitive satisfaction at its ultimate levels may require analysis in terms that include the *whole* man's quest for understanding, i.e., not only the defeat of disconnection through logical coherence among our concepts but the victory over arbitrariness as well.

Is this, though, to embark upon a journey without hope of arrival—or worse, as Hospers tells us—to begin a search for the answer to a senseless question? What "answer" could *possibly*, in principle, satisfy the insatiable demand? Would we recognize the answer if we found it? On the plane of pure theory, let it be repeated, there can be no such answer, no such "arrival," no such satisfaction. In theory it is possible to go on asking the question "Why?" as Hospers says, forever.

The notion of the arbitrary needs further inspection, however, for its poignancy extends beyond the theoretical domain. We tend to be bothered by the arbitrary when confronted with that which seems either void of meaning or downright *wrong* (note the overtones of the phrase "brute fact"). Whatever is *right* or valuable, on the other hand, needs no further justification for its being. Our ultimate cognitive resting-place as men— whole men who are valuers and agents as well as thinkers—would seem to lie nowhere short of that elusive point where ultimate *fact* is seen also as perfect *good*, where our most reliable account of "the way things are" shows also the ultimate *rightness* of things. Such rightness, of course, is properly predicable only of the *whole* state of affairs referred to in our ultimate explanations. It would be not only methodologically self-defeating but also logically a category-mistake to characterize partial or proximate explanations as though they were ultimate ones. We can allow no shortcut to the termination of the cognitive process through premature appeals to value considerations; but, equally, we shall find no cognitively satisfying termination of this process at all, apart from a vision of the whole of whatever *is* as also that which *ought* to be.

But wait a moment! If we adopt this view, are we not in danger of begging the question about the character of reality as a whole? To say that explanations of unlimited generality *must* show the "rightness of things" in order to avoid the irrationality of arbitrariness may, at first glance, seem to be a blatant *petitio* concerning what may be the case. Such a supposition, however, would be mistaken. There is no claim made here that any logically coherent and experientially grounded explanation of unlimited generality *will* in fact exhibit the unity of *is* with *ought*. It may even be that constructing a conceptual synthesis, relevant to the for-

---

[34]Cf. Bendall and Ferré, *Exploring the Logic of Faith.*

midable (and growing) mass of contemporary knowledge, undigested, incoherent, and unstable as it is—a conceptual synthesis, in other words, that succeeds merely in overcoming the single enemy of disconnection— may alone prove (though perfectly legitimate in principle) practically impossible at the present moment in history. And even if, by dint of generous efforts from geniuses as yet unknown, a fortunate model should prove fruitful in the development of such an omnirelevant account of things as we have in mind, it would still *remain to be seen* whether this account answered man's nontheoretic (practical and valuational) thirst for explanatory satisfaction. It may be that the arbitrary, at the furthest reaches of our conceptions, will never be eliminated from the human situation. But if so, this is a discovery to be made, not an axiom to be assumed. And inasmuch as the arbitrary *is* ever genuinely overcome in cognition (as is the present writer's contention), the palm will go to the ultimate explanation that combines the unsparing standards of theoretical success with the fruitful satisfaction of human aspiration.

It is here that we discover again the profound insight into the human cognitive situation displayed by such giants of conceptual synthesis as Plato, Aristotle, or Spinoza. In each of their attempts at offering ultimate explanations the Real is inseparable from the Right; the *is* and the *ought* are seen *sub specie aeternitatis*, one and the same. The arbitrary is overcome; brute fact is seen not to be just "brutal" but to display a necessity that is also acceptable; the demand for understanding comes, for a time at least, to fulfillment.

Plato, Aristotle, and Spinoza will not, of course, satisfy our conceptual needs today. The concepts that they were attempting to bring into coherent relation are not our own; human knowledge, thanks very largely to the spectacular successes of the special sciences, has vastly increased. It is our own knowledge, not the concepts of an earlier day, that we demand to see "steadily and whole." But these thinkers, though chosen only as examples, are properly of more than antiquarian interest. Their diagnosis of the cognitive demand was basically correct, although their specific prescriptions for its treatment no longer satisfy. In thus stressing the *continuing* nature of the quest for ultimate explanations—frankly recognizing these to be corrigible, like their distinguished forerunners—we embark upon this philosophic enterprise perhaps more adequately forewarned concerning the logical character of our task. Just as long as human knowledge continues to grow and human judgment to develop, so long will the search for fresh and fuller syntheses be required. The cognitive demand for ultimate explanations is not a threat, therefore, to the wholesome excitement of the hunt. The satisfactions of the search are no less genuine than the pleasures of possession. Ultimate explanation in our interpretation is no enemy, then, to free minds; instead, the common enemies of responsible thought at all levels are dogmatism, prejudice, and that un-adventuresome temper so bound by orthodoxies, and by what Hume called modes, as to shun the risks always present in creative "venturing far out." Every ultimate explanation, religious or secular, is an invitation to take a chance.

VI.   THEOLOGICAL EXPLANATION
IN TERMS OF PURPOSE

Finally, we may at last explicitly consider the status of theological explanation in the light of what has been maintained. In a sense, those are right who scornfully curl a logical lip at explanations of the nature of things *via* appeals to "God's purpose." It is true, as far as we can tell from anthropology and studies of infant logic, that animism and the attempt to account for all things in terms of purpose are, as Hospers tells us, the most primitive conceptions of explanation.[35] But the case may not be left on this level. If ultimate explanation, to be cognitively satisfying, demands in principle a union of fact and value, the explanatory model of a perfectly good personal purpose joined to creative sovereignty over all being may —if, *but only if*, it is rigorously articulated, coherently and illuminatingly related to all knowledge and experience, and successfully defended against prima facie incoherences—deserve our philosophical attention and respect. The fact that explanations in terms of purposes are ubiquitous would then prove to be significant for positive as well as for negative reasons. The most primitive concept of explanation is, perhaps, best qualified to be our ultimate basis for explanation as well! Just as familiarity may be seen after all to reflect the victory over disconnection, so also purpose in the last analysis may turn out to represent our most effective weapon against arbitrariness.

If this is so, however, it will not be so because of the appeal of *purpose* alone or even primarily, but because purpose, taken as an explanatory model, proves capable both of undergirding a successfully coherent conceptual synthesis and of being recognized as *good*. In a footnote of his discussion of the blank contingency of ultimate explanations, Hospers writes:

> Explanation in terms of divine purposes again will not help: if we are told that the laws of nature are as they are because God willed it so, we can ask why He should have willed it so; and if here again an answer is given, we can once again ask a why-question of this answer.[36]

[35]Hospers, "What Is Explanation?" p. 95.
[36]Ibid., p. 117.

Who is to tell Hospers that he is wrong here? Of course one can do as he describes, asking over and over again the theoretical "Why?" or rejecting every stopping place as theoretically arbitrary. But to shift the emphasis so that theological explanation is seen not so much in terms of "divine *purpose*" as "purpose that is *divine*"—and to understand the "divine" as that which is worthy of our worship—this (or something of this *kind*) may conceivably offer a way through which men can responsibly cope with the cognitive bottomlessness of the arbitrary.

Those who take the procedures and practical aims of the special sciences as determinative for all respectable cognitive endeavor will in all likelihood be shocked by this injection of value consideration into the notion of explanation and hence into cognition. There is little recognized room in the methodology of the special sciences for consideration of value—at least when it comes to choosing between proffered explanatory schemes. The franchise of the scientist is vast but not carte blanche. It is to give us understanding for the sake of coping with nature, and for this pursuit our role as valuers remains normally and methodologically subordinate (though not entirely inactive, as witnessed by the importance of such aesthetic values as "elegance" and such practical values as "simplicity," in our decisions between scientific theories).

The franchise of the philosopher is also to provide us with "understanding," but not alone for the sake of coping with nature. The postanalytical, ecologically aware philosopher who determines to move carefully, self-consciously, and rigorously toward synthesis will attempt to construct—not only with the aid of the specialized scientist but also with the aid of the artist, the moralist, the theologian, the man of affairs, and the poet—a coherent and effective conceptual context within which he and other men may cope with *all* of their environment and the *totality* of their experience, including felt demands of value and of action. To deny philosophers the right to engage in this synthesizing explanatory activity is to deny ourselves, and others, the possibility of substituting a rational and responsible for an irrational and irresponsible means of coping with life as a whole and the earth as a whole.

Finally, the theologian deserves to be drawn back once again into his rightful place in the thoughtful community. If my account is correct, it is only the theologian disciplined by science and philosophy—or the philosopher prepared to venture into the theological domain of ultimate value commitments—who will bring the cognitive quest to whatever approximate completion may be hoped for by any generation. It may be that the current situation is ill suited to our generation's hopes of cognitive satisfaction; it may be that synthesis is less needed (or possible) in turbulent times than is a constant alertness to the ever-changing data—data of value as well as of empirical belief. But if the human spirit continues, as seems likely, to demand ultimate explanations, we shall at least be in a position to ask certain crucial questions of any candidate for our acceptance. First, is this proposed explanation in keeping with the best findings of the special sciences, whose explanatory models and theories lie at the beginning of the quest for understanding and may not be ignored without cognitive peril? Second, has the candidate for explanation overcome the disconnection of separate explanatory paradigms in the various special sciences by some coherent principle of theoretical unification that is also adequately inclusive? And, finally, has the value dimension of human life been seriously considered and tested against humanity's most profound intuitions of ultimate worth? It is by these criteria, I submit, that a theology of nature must be evaluated. The functions of scientist, philosopher, and theologian in explanation are not identical; they are, I believe, continuous. Therefore if we continue to hope for understanding as whole men, we shall wish success to each.

FREDERICK FERRÉ is Charles A. Dana Professor of
Philosophy at Dickinson College, where he teaches
philosophy of science, philosophy of religion, metaphysics,
and epistemology. He is the author of Language, Logic
and God *and* Basic Modern Philosophy of Religion *and*
coauthor of Exploring the Logic of Faith. *He edited*
Paley's Natural Theology *and* Comte's Introduction to
Positive Philosophy *and has published essays on the*
philosophy of science, the philosophy of religion, and other
topics.

JOHN J. COMPTON

3
Science and
God's Action
in Nature

One of the things our present environmental problems demand of us is that we reassess our fundamental attitudes toward nature. As scientific analysis, technological control, and city life have grown, most of us have left behind the elemental view of nature as the living source and home of man. We treat nature as a self-contained physical system, a resource to be exploited, or a colorful relief from a largely artificial environment. The gains in useful knowledge have been immense. But we are now being forced to see how incomplete these more modern perspectives on nature are. We have paid insufficient attention to our dependence on nature; we have not understood the environmental effects of what we do. And the result is that we have not respected the integrity of man and nature.

To restore that respect demands more than increased knowledge; it requires that we affirm intrinsic meaning and value in the natural order of which man is a part. But is such an affirmation possible and intelligible today? This is a profound question for men living in a scientific world. Can the concepts of creation and providence, of the intrinsic purposiveness and goodness of the created world, any longer be held concomitantly with the determination to pursue scientific understanding as far as it will go?

Is a theology of nature incompatible with natural science? Is there an inherent conflict between theistic belief and the scientific account of the world? It has often seemed so. In order to accommodate scientific truth, it has often appeared necessary to abandon the view that God creates or that he acts in nature, or else to limit scientific explanation of nature severely in favor of theistic belief. We have only to remember Galileo and the Inquisition, and Darwin and the monkey trials.

But how did such conflicts develop? Recall, for example, the situation in 1610, when the professors are said to have refused to look through Galileo's new telescope at the moons of Jupiter.[1] The fault did not lie so much in religious obstinacy as in scientific and philosophic caution. Being well-educated, systematic thinkers and gifted with common sense, these men—even if they had looked—would probably not have seen what Galileo saw. Why so? Because one typically sees what one is looking for. And it was obvious to everyone in those days that the sun and stars, like the moon, moved around the earth. So did the planets, although in a somewhat more complex way. Besides, a well-developed astronomy could predict the positions of these moving "lights" on the same basis. Aristotle's physics also explained why these objects stayed out there and did not fall: they were made of special matter (ether) and traveled about on concentric etherial spheres. Beyond the outermost sphere was the heaven of God. His constant providential action was manifest in the movement and harmony of the whole. Thus theology was provided for. Space and human destiny mirrored one another; man's salvation was God's central concern, so man's earth was at the center of space. And from the earth, man could look upward and outward to a less earthly, celestial region that pointed beyond itself to God.

The symmetry and coherence of this philosophical-scientific-theological picture was immense. The proof is that we still think in terms of it in many ways. It was this vision of the whole, this grand conceptual scheme, not the Christian faith, that Copernicus and Galileo challenged. And it took more than a few glimpses of spots of light through a lens tube to undermine it. It took a wholly new physics and philosophy of physics, the end of which is not even in sight yet. The issue was not really the authority of Scripture, although it came to this in the minds of some. The issue was the authority of the conceptual scheme that had been used to interpret the Bible. And it was this conceptual scheme that the new scientific thinking repudiated as an ultimate authority.[2]

Since the task of interpretation and reinterpretation—of relating faith to the best available scientific knowledge—seems inescapable, so are the

[1]See Thomas Kuhn, *The Copernican Revolution* (New York: Random House, Inc., 1959), and also his *Structure of Scientific Revolutions*, 2nd ed. (Chicago: University of Chicago Press, Phoenix Books, 1970).

[2]For this history, see John Dillenberger, *Protestant Thought and Natural Science* (New York: Doubleday & Company, Inc., 1960), especially Chaps. 1–3.

changes and conflicts that go with it. One perennial difficulty lies in our false expectation that science will find God for us—if not "out there beyond the stars," then somehow directly at work in the particular changes of nature. This interpretation of divine Providence was one basis for the resistance, in the nineteenth century, to Lyell's developmental geology and to Darwin's theory of the natural selection of animal species.[3]

For what these men did was to show, in effect, that God is not needed as an hypothesis to explain the origins of things in nature. Mountains and rock strata were not created in their present form, but were produced by the regular action of heat, pressure, sedimentation, and erosion over millions of years. During part of this time, and subsequently, animal species have appeared and disappeared, not by special creation or destruction, but again by natural process—by evolution from simpler forms through genetic variation, the struggle for survival, and selection of the best adapted. Through a similar operation of natural causes man was born and we now believe, so was life itself.

In the light of such historic conflicts, must we infer that God is irrelevant to nature? Not at all. The point is rather that we now have to view God's action quite differently.

I. THE AUTONOMY OF NATURE

There are several important lessons involved in the recognition that God does not serve as an acceptable explanation of any particular change in nature. First, there is the autonomy of natural science. Methodologically, we are bound to affirm that whatever questions can be posed scientifically about natural events are to be answered scientifically in terms of natural events. Science necessarily depersonalizes and divests nature of its divinization, considering it apart from its creative source, in order to study it. The shift in our concepts of space and time from closed, personalized structures to boundless and impersonal ones, is still continuing for most of us.

Second, there is the acknowledgement of the nonphysical character of God—i.e., that God is not up there pushing the stars around. He is not a being *alongside* the world, or *before* the world, acting on it in particular ways and times, and this is precisely why he is not available as a factor in scientific explanations. What this recognition amounts to is that the "classical model"—or, perhaps, better, the "pop-classical model"—of God as the

[3]Charles G. Gillispie, *Genesis and Geology* (Cambridge: Harvard University Press, 1951), and John C. Greene, *The Death of Adam* (New York: The New American Library, Inc., 1961).

thinglike manipulator has had to be given up. But this is sheer gain, for this lesson is just what the tradition of biblical piety and religious devotion has always tried to proclaim.

But this gain in illumination has at the same time left an enormous vacuum in religious thought. For no model of God adequate to replace the pop-classical model is readily forthcoming. Having been removed from "out there in physical space" by Galileo and Copernicus, and from "back then" or even "here, now" in time by Lyell and Darwin, it appears that God is not only no-thing, but is in fact nothing. Lacking any model of God's transcendence except the discredited spatial one, it is easy to drop this transcendence entirely from view.

Third, then, what began to happen, as the naturalistic vision of an autonomous nature grew in power in the eighteenth and nineteenth centuries, was that *human* experience replaced *natural* experience in having significance for theology. The imperiousness of moral experience, or the sense of man's ultimate dependence and contingency, or the sense of the sacred and saving in historical events, became clues to understanding the meaning of God in the religious sense. Existentialist motifs in more recent years have virtually preempted the field: the meaning of God is to be found in the human search for meaning in life; a man's God is his object of ultimate concern; and a true or adequate religious belief is one that, in the fullest sense, satisfies the human drive for meaning, for openness, for freedom, for affirmation of self and world.

Now I am far from disparaging this third consequence. It *is* the case that the starting point of biblical religion lies in man's confrontation—beyond his world of impotence, suffering, and guilt—with something "more" that empowers him to love, to hope, and to grow. There *is* a restricted sense of religious truth, as described by Paul Tillich, in which a religious affirmation is true if it expresses an authentically renewed, life-affirming existence on man's part. It is existentially true. But this is simply not enough. Man is a being in a natural world that is open to natural science as well. His world is conditioned by the world of nature; his history is enveloped by cosmic history. No religious affirmation can be fully meaningful to us today, much less true, unless it relates us and our concept of God to that natural world and to cosmic history. We need a more adequate concept of God the creator and sustainer, God the agent in nature, than we currently possess.

Historically, there have been many candidates for this job, from the scholastic Infinite Being and Pure Act, through the Hegelian Absolute, to Tillich's Ground of Being, Whitehead's Evolving and Suffering Companion, and Teilhard's Omega Point. I do not have a full metaphysical system to offer, however, nor do I wish to examine the credentials of each of these candidates. What I would like to try is something more modest, namely, to suggest in terms of ordinary experience what a satisfactory concept of God might be like.

It strikes me that our chief difficulty lies not so much in inventing conceptual models as in giving them plausibility and applicability—that is, in making them believable, both in terms of our common experience and in terms of the scientific world view. It is this test of plausibility and applicability—ultimately of coherence with the rest of our knowledge—that is the inclusive test of truth for religious affirmation. We have to ask not only whether one who affirms the reality of a creative and loving God has successfully conquered his self-alienation and sense of meaninglessness, but whether the concept of God can any longer be explicated so as to illuminate the natural world as we know it in ordinary experience and in science.[4] This question must be answered if we are to defend a theology of nature which can support an ecological ethic today.

II. THE LANGUAGE OF ACTION AND AGENCY

What would it be like to say that God creates or that God guides or that God acts in nature? Let me consider an analogy from common life: I move my arm. What can be said about this phenomenon?

In the first place, from the scientific or naturalistic view, this movement is a succession of *events* linked together causally in my body. These events may be described and explained as completely as is desired. And yet, from the agent's view (my view) or from yours, this happening constitutes not merely a series of movements or specific bodily events, but an *action*: it may be a signal, or a wave, a gesture of illustration, a yawn, a stretch, and so on. But in any case, it is an action, or it is perceived as having the form of an action. This is, I suggest, a primary datum in the context of personal relations. And, what is most instructive, my arm motion is an action *at the same time*, if not in the same respect, in which it is a succession of causally linked events. Between these two perspectives there is no conflict whatsoever.

As an action, this arm motion is made what it is, not by the particular physical events that transpire in it, but by the purpose or intent that it expresses. Any given action—say, yawning, illustrating, pointing, or mailing a letter—may be variously performed, that is, performed with different specific movements involving different causal processes. On the other

---

[4]For a full background to this question in current philosophical theology, see Ian G. Barbour, *Issues in Science and Religion* (Englewood Cliffs, N.J.: Prentice-Hall, Inc., 1966), especially Chaps. 12–13.

hand, similar events and processes may condition quite different actions; for example, the movements of the fingers, hand, and arm, and presumably of the nervous system, in dealing a card and in posting a letter, are virtually the same, although the actions are unlike. This suggests that the analysis of actions reveals a different structure and system of relations from the analysis of bodily events. An act becomes part of other acts, not as an event causing them, or caused by them, but as a subphase of an inclusive intent or purpose. I illustrate in order to make a point, I make the point in order to complete an argument, I complete an argument in order to make a speech, I speak in order to edify, to inform, or to aggravate, and so on and on. Whereas bodily events sustain causal connections in space and time, the same events, viewed as an action, sustain relations, in a means-ends continuum, with other and more inclusive actions. Similarly, whereas events simply *are* what they are, actions are always subject to appraisal and criticism as justified or unjustified, intelligent or unwise, risky, precipitous, or perhaps unclear, in so far as the relevant purposes are or are not realized in the relevant ways. Thus, the entire logic of bodily events and the logic of actions—each equally applicable to me and my behavior—are different.[5]

In the second place, there is an *agent* of an action, not just events that happen. *I* move my arm. There is *someone* who illustrates, gestures, points, yawns, speaks, and so on. But, and this is the crucial point, this agent is not another cause *alongside* the bodily behavior. I act *through* moving my arm or *by* moving my arm; *I* do not act upon a nerve cell and thence on a muscle, and thence on a bone, as Descartes seems to have thought. My *nerve cell* does effect a change in my muscle and in my bone position, and so on, to be sure, but *I*, the agent, am not another entity in *that* series or influencing that series by discrete and occult forces of another sort. *I* am my living body in action, not two things—myself plus my body, my body plus a cause behind the scenes—but my body as active, as agent. My body, the same body, is both a conditioned and conditioning process of causally linked events and a purposing, intending subject of action, without there being any mystery at all why it can be this way.

And yet, at the same time, viewing my "self" as agent, *I transcend* any single action, even the ensemble of actions completed or to be completed by me. I am never fully expressed in my actions, not even in my speech acts, my efforts at direct communication. It is common experience that our intentions may be hidden not only from other persons but also, at

[5]See A. I. Melden, *Free Action* (London: Routledge & Kegan Paul, Ltd., 1961). Recent discussions of this point and of other related issues in the theory of action may be found in Norman Care and Charles Landesman's *Readings in the Theory of Action* (Bloomington: Indiana University Press, 1968), and Alan R. White's *The Philosophy of Action* (London: Oxford University Press, 1968).

least in part, from ourselves. Some intentions are too inchoate, some too complex, some too frightening, some too far reaching for you or me to discern. I often have to interpret what I am doing and saying for you; I have to reveal myself to you, and yet even this may be insufficient and incomplete. This is because I transcend my expressions to you, both in depth and toward the future.

III. GOD AS AGENT:
A MODEL

With this very brief description of our common experience of personal action before us, we may turn to its suggestiveness for understanding divine action. I believe there is a certain analogy between the relation of an agent to the bodily movements that express his action, and the relation of God as agent to the movements of nature and history.[6]

In the first place, we can distinguish the causal development of events from the meaning of these events viewed as God's action. Scientific analysis of physical nature and of human history has no more need of God as an explanatory factor than the physiologist needs my conscious intent to explain my bodily movements. Nor does God need to find a "gap" in nature in order to act, any more than you or I need a similar interstice in our body chemistry. Each story has a complete cast of characters, without the need for interaction with the other story, but quite compatible with it. What happens is that the evolution of things is *seen* or *read*, in religious life—as my arm's movement is read in individual life—as a part of an action, as an expression of divine purpose, in addition to its being viewed as a naturalistic process.

In the second place, as before, the agent is not alongside his actions. God is not alongside the world, inserting himself into it at special moments, any more than I am behind or alongside my bodily life. He lives *through* the history of nature as I live through my body. He *is* that history, just as I *am* my body, and yet he is not exhausted in it. He is that history without being identical with any individual part or event in it. As with human agents, he too transcends the particular behavioral expressions we see, with hidden, complex, and inclusive purposes of his own. The central

[6]In this section and the next, I draw heavily upon ideas developed by Gordon D. Kaufman in his "Two Models of Transcendence," *The Heritage of Christian Thought*, eds. R. E. Cushman and E. Grislis (New York: Harper & Row, Publishers, 1965) and in his "Transcendence without Mythology," *Harvard Theological Review*, 1966, reprinted in *New Theology No. 4*, eds. M. Marty and Dean Peerman (New York: The Macmillan Company, 1967). Cf. also John B. Cobb, Jr., *A Christian Natural Theology* (Philadelphia: The Westminster Press, 1965).

point is that the sense of God's personal transcendence, if we model it on the personal transcendence of the embodied, finite, and personal agent, does *not* require a radical dualism between God and the physical world.

What I have sketched here is no panacea. As David Hume showed us, analogies from the world to God are thin reeds indeed. I have in no way argued that there is *evidence* for the existence of God in cosmic history. Nor is it lost on me that recognizing any parts of cosmic history as parts of the action of God—that is, interpreting their significance in his purposes—is a treacherous business at best, infinitely more so than interpreting the actions of men. Although we are able to distinguish and interpret discrete human actions, there is in a sense only *one* all-embracing divine action of creation-judgment-salvation. We thus lack the customary context within which we have learned to view the actions of men—namely, a context in which we can draw parallels among their different actions, distinguish periods of their different types of activity, and communicate with them about their actions in a common language. And yet even here we are not entirely without some analogies; for, to the sympathetic eye, there is in the cosmic drama viewed as divine activity a kind of pattern, offering its constants, its distinguishable phases, and at least a gestural language.

IV.   GOD AS AGENT:
LIMITATIONS OF THE MODEL

In addition to these difficulties of application, however, there are more serious theoretical limitations to our analogy. Such limitations have to be expected; most theoretical models in the sciences—for example, those of atomic and nuclear structure—have to be qualified and supplemented by still other models that express other features of the phenomena. In our case, the limitations are of two sorts: the limited adequacy of our understanding of human action, on the one hand, and in its limited applicability to divine activity, on the other.

My key to understanding human action has been my ordinary experience of it and language about it; this suggests a view of the person as essentially one, an embodied subject acting through but not on his body. According to this view, what a person does is open, consistently, both to a physiological-causal analysis when considered as bodily movement, and to a more inclusive, functional-intentional analysis when considered as purposive action. Personal transcendence is a transcendence-in-immanence; it is that characteristic of an agent whose experiences and purposes are always bodily motivated but never fully developed or expressed.

Now it is plainly the case that the ordinary concept of human action is *not* so unambiguously incarnational. In fact, our bodies seem frequently to be marginal, even opposed, to our true selves. We speak of struggling against ourselves; we seek often to restrain bodily impulses; we aim to discipline and to establish control over our bodies. We see many things happening in and to our bodies that have no intrinsic action-meaning at all—such as coughs, injuries, and sickness. And, above all, we see ourselves as *free from* bodily conditions in a more radical sense—free to imagine, to weigh, and thus to intend and pursue novel alternatives. We take ourselves to be *free to modify* bodily conditions in a way that would be inexplicable from the standpoint of a purely physiological-causal analysis. From at least the time of Plato, this more dualistic, interactionist model of the person has seemed to many to be inescapable. It entails an incompleteness in principle for any physiological explanation of bodily movement; and, interestingly, it has typically been accompanied by a more dualistic, inter-actionist understanding of the relation between God and the world.

However, it has proved virtually impossible to articulate this dualist view clearly, to say what this separate self or mind might be and how it evolves with, is conditioned by, and acts on the body. And at every step of the way, the view risks implications that would be at variance with physiological knowledge—e.g., claims that certain bodily occurrences, or types of occurrences, have no sufficient bodily conditions. The most prom-ising course seems thus to be to retain the incarnational perspective and to refine it; our bodies are more complex self-regulatory systems than we thought. No doubt we struggle to discipline our bodily impulses, to control reflex and sickness, and to imagine and pursue freely chosen ends. But these are possibilities for us precisely in virtue of, not in spite of, our bodily constitution. Consciously held reasons and intentions *are* causes of our actions, and they do effectively modify bodily conditions. But this is not inexplicable physiologically; it is true because these reasons and inten-tions have a basis in certain complex states of our brains and nervous systems that may, on principle, be analyzed. I believe, in short, that our best hope for an adequate concept of the person will be found by holding firmly to the *irreducibility* of human thought and action and yet also to the *constant basis of* such thought and action *in* bodily states and proc-esses.[7]

Even if we suppose, however, that such a concept of the person is going to be adequate, there remain very serious *theological* limitations of our analogy between human agency and divine agency. These center in the fact that whereas *I* act in and through my body as a *controlling* agent,

[7]See Jerry Fodor, *Psychological Explanation* (New York: Random House, Inc., 1968), especially Chap. 3.

God elicits from nature a human community with which he enters into *social*, and not primarily controlling, relations. *Human* history is not appropriately viewed as God's body. For this reason, our model needs to be replaced by a more interpersonal one when God's relation to human beings and to human history is at stake. The biblical analogies—God as father, as king, as shepherd, and the like—all express this. These models of God's action in human history have a much more social character, one that respects man's freedom *from God*, his responsibility for his own actions and his dependence on God's personal (not controlling) presence for reconciliation. One's body does not have that kind of independent, personal life.

At the same time, there are hints of it. For example, my body does indeed have a life of its own. And this control of my body is precisely *not* a "manipulative" control. The body contains processes, physiological cycles, unlearned reflexes, and the like, that are mine, but only involuntarily so. These give the body a "wisdom" of its own, upon which I depend, for which I must care, and which I may adopt and adapt, at best, but never completely rule. In a similar way, the elements and laws of physical nature, although they are God's, may be thought to be independent of him, and individual physical events may be viewed as independent of his actions. Not everything that occurs in nature is an act of God any more than everything that occurs in (or to) me is my act. However, the patterned recurrence of events is the *basis* of any expressive actions appearing at all. In this way also, just as I need my body, so God needs the physical world as a means of expression. My body resists instantaneous translation of thought into action, with the result that I have a life, a persistence over time and through space, and a mode of entry into a world that I may share with others. The meaning of my body for me suggests what has long been seen as the meaning of physical nature for God, a nature through which he constitutes himself and is constituted as a social being. This is because it is the physical world that gives individuality, distance, and independence to men. Far from being incompatible with the personal, reconciling role God plays as guide for free men in history, his bodily life in nature is its adumbration and precondition.

But although God needs the world as a means of creating a community with men, he does not need it absolutely. *The* crucial theological shortcoming of our model is that it fails to convey the radical transcendence and freedom of God with respect to natural and human history. Although it illuminates the immanence of God in all history, it fails to deal with the absolutely first and last things—with creation and culmination. What human action represents is transcendence-in-immanence; this is the way a person transcends his bodily life. But the God of the biblical tradition is a god experienced as perfect, as the one supreme and holy will, the one true object of worship and loyalty, and the one everlasting basis of hope. The sense that nothing can finally defeat the purposes and love of God requires the concept of the *super*-natural. It is religious hope, not spatial relations, that gives this concept its meaning. A god thus understood must have absolute power and goodness, must create in a radical sense (from nothing), must endure if human culture and even if the earth itself be destroyed, and must be free to try again, if need be, in order to achieve his purposes. Such transcendence exceeds the conceptual limits of any analogy with embodied human action. I do not create my body, and I do not outlive it.

And yet it is necessary to urge that *both* transcendence-in-immanence *and* radical transcendence be retained in order to do justice to the religious phenomenon of radical faith and hope. Even if religious hope is in God and not in nature or man, it still affirms that what is created is not wasted and contains potentialities for new life and new relationships. The Christian God affirms this world and human history. Although he might not, yet he does in fact choose this natural order and chooses to live through it, much as our analogy suggests, in order to make human life possible, and he chooses to help renew that human life in order to make it meaningful.

These reflections do not constitute a rigorous argument. All I really intend to argue at this point is that, as a *part* of our attempt to give a plausible conceptualization of God's relation to the physical world, the analogy with embodied human action bears serious meditation. The more one meditates about it, I am convinced, the more its suggestiveness is apparent. It is at least *consistent* with Christian faith and tradition at most points and may even be (a stronger claim) *coherent* with natural science and the scientific world view. I want now, as a final step, to begin to make out this last claim.

V.   THE NEW UNDERSTANDING
OF NATURE

The chief problem that has plagued theistic analysis of the natural world is the apparent impossibility of any divine action in a completely causal natural order. What the exploration of the analogy with human action suggests is that this is, in fact, no problem. For just as a human bodily movement is or may be causally conditioned in its physical linkage, although remaining an intentional action with full meaning, so also a causally determined cosmic history may be an expressive action of God. The history of nature may or may not be completely causal (it almost certainly is not), but this is not the point. The complete abandonment of the interactionist, pop-classical model of God and the world makes it clear, as we saw, that God does not have to find an interstice in the chemical or physiological reactions of the world in order to make something happen, any more than you or I do.

On the other hand, there *were* characteristics of the seventeenth- and eighteenth-century descriptions of nature that did conflict with inter- preting the world process as expression of a divine purpose—namely, the essentially repetitive, static, and exceedingly simple, materialistic char- acter that nature seemed to possess. As long as nature seemed reduced to a directionless and simple materialistic scheme, divine action, if present at all, could at best appear rudimentary and without importance. Deism, then, was a plausible response and a correlate to the dominant (Cartesian) view of animals as automata and men as automata propelled by resident, separate souls.

Yet there can be little doubt that the operative concept of nature among practicing natural scientists has undergone a critical transformation over the past 50 years, and it had already begun to change in the nine- teenth century. We are dealing with a regulative idea, to be sure. But to judge from the works of astronomers, physicists, and biologists, although written with different emphases and idioms, there has appeared a general concept of nature that is distinctive in at least three respects.[8]

The earlier, largely Newtonian view had found nature to be (1) *simple in structure*—therefore readily reducible to the patterns of combi- nation of a few elementary components; (2) *mechanically determined in behavior*—therefore predictable with precision from any given state with the aid of causal laws; and (3) *static in form*—entirely without funda- mental novelty or change in structure, closed, and thus exhibiting laws of all-embracing scope in space and time.

The current concept, on the contrary, finds nature to be quite dif- ferent from the Newtonian view in all three respects. In the first place, nature is now seen to be *enormously complex*. It now shows many levels of order—each with its own distinctive forms and irreducible laws, with many types of elements at these levels, and with an increasing rather than decreasing multiplicity of questions to be asked as the inquiry proceeds. Consider what has happened to the concept of matter alone. Not long ago physicists thought that matter was quite distinct from light and that atomic theory, together with gravitation and the laws of motion, could account for all of physical dynamics. The discoveries of radioactivity and X-rays and the study of atomic and nuclear structure shattered this expec- tation. Although group theory arranges them in a pattern, we now have thirty or more "elementary" particles (the "Zoo" increases every day)

---

[8]See Harold Schilling's contribution to the present volume (Chap. 7).

with a variety of physical attributes—positively or negatively charged, long- or short-lived, right- or left-handed spin, with a variety of states— now like particles, now like waves, now fused, now transmuted. Chemical and biological studies, moreover, reveal many types of entities composed of these microphysical constituents—enormously varied molecules, chains of molecules, crystals, genes, chromosomes, cell nuclei, protoplasm, cells, organs, organisms, and so on, to say nothing of larger bodies like the earth, planetary systems, and galaxies. Our knowledge here is far reaching; there *is* an astonishing order, but it is not the oversimple order we once saw.

The current view, in the second place, finds nature far from strictly causally determined. It appears rather to be a *field of chance and of statistical as well as causal uniformity.* This development has been most dramatic within physics, with the advent of quantum theory and the indeterminacy relations. Most physicists and philosophers of physics seem to agree (although they may not like the fact) that present theory implies that objectively, and in fact, material particles of very small dimensions do not possess precise values of physical variables, except under special conditions. They cannot, in any case, possess certain combinations of these precise values simultaneously. Their character is such, and the laws of quantum theory are such, that their individual behavior is not theoretically determinate; the laws of quantum theory prescribe statistical regularities of aggregates of similar microphysical systems only. And although macroscopic beings are "classical" in most physical respects, biology, psychology, and the social sciences reveal such a dominance of statistical modes of behavior in their own right that it seems clear that *actual* nature, at many levels, responds to so many conditions that to speak of mechanically determined behavior at any level is at best a useful abstraction.

Finally, the recent view of nature finds it far from static. On the contrary, nature appears to be a *historical field of evolving forms, inexhaustible in its potential for change and open to the future.* This conclusion seems to follow not only from the geological, biological, and human sciences but from physical science as well. It is a significant point of agreement within contemporary astronomy that the physical universe exhibits a history (whether cyclic or linear remains to be seen) along which atoms come into being, explosion or expansion of the matter-cloud takes place, galaxies are formed, suns condense, solar systems evolve—perhaps thousands of millions of them—with earths somewhat like our own and, perhaps, with living beings similar to ourselves inhabiting them. The history of nature, in other words, does seem to be a reality—each form of system, with its laws, succeeding the other, permitted by it, revealing new potential within it—the potential for life and mind, for example—and containing within it the potential for an as yet unknown future. The very tempo of this change, moreover, seems to have increased with time.

VI. GOD'S ACTION
IN NATURE

Now *this nature*, complex and many-leveled, partly causal and partly not, evolving historically with man inseparably a part and phase of its development, is what contemporary natural science presents for our belief. And it is my thesis that this cosmic view is profoundly *coherent* with Christian theism, at least with a theism that understands God as an agent in the sense I have sketched.

How can this be seen? First, from the position of Christian theism, this new scientific view of nature can hardly fail to put content into such questions as "What does it mean that God creates?" or "What does it mean that God acts in nature?" These questions do not seek special, secret knowledge of the intimate and private life of a being behind the scenes. Rather, the meaning of divine action is to be found, if at all, not simply through a reading of human "salvation history," but also through a serious and sympathetic reading of the quality and direction of natural history. To say that God acts in nature means that *just the sort of dynamic, creative, novelty-producing evolution that takes place does take place*. It means in part that through all the eons of historical movement, even in erratic or wasteful moments, the long-range developmental curve has a direction. This direction has consistently been toward complexity, organization, consciousness, and sociality—at least, within the limited region of the known universe. The magnificence of the ordered complexity of the history of nature, as science knows it, can therefore, and still should, excite the wonder and admiration of men for its creative and sustaining source.

At the same time, however, as this view of nature is coherent with a theistic understanding of its meaning, it underscores the *limits* of what we may say of God and thereby reveals our "learned ignorance" concerning him. I say this because it has been clear from the beginning of the science-theology confrontation that the chief source of confusion in this great debate has been the inveterate human tendency to spatialize and temporalize God—to put him outside or alongside the universe, or to place him before it in time or acting at specific moments upon it. We have seen that when this is done, God becomes an addendum to the world, and the postulation of his action as explanation of natural events becomes scientifically preposterous, philosophically naive, and theologically idolatrous. My point here is that the newer concept of nature—as distinct from the older, simplistic, and static concept—can help to remind us of the true mystery, openness, and limitations of our knowledge of God. This is true, not because God is an absolutely hidden being of inscrutable will, but rather, in the terms of our analogy, because his worldly expression in nature, his activity itself, is so rich and difficult to interpret. The modern view of the creation, the vast historical process, dynamic and complex, should serve to curb the pretensions of those claiming to locate God precisely or to determine his nature and purposes with great certainty. Such claims cannot be made of God if they cannot be made for nature, his creation, itself!

Moreover, this view of nature permits the suggestion that God is not, as we are not, an absolutely controlling agent who is simply incompletely *revealed* in bodily action. He is, as we are, *in fact incomplete*, incomplete in knowledge of and control over natural bodily history. He depends, as we do, on that history—on its relatively independent structures, possibilities, and developing habits of life. "He really does go out of himself to participate in, to suffer with, and to move through the world's history to a fulfillment even he does not fully know or control."[9] If this is the social meaning of God's life in the world—and surely this is affirmed to be so for God's life in human history—then it is significant that this relationship is foreshadowed in God's primordial relation to nature itself.

JOHN J. COMPTON is Professor of Philosophy and Chairman of the Department of Philosophy at Vanderbilt University. He has written for various philosophical journals and has contributed to such volumes as Phenomenology in America *(edited by James Edie) and* Boston Studies in Philosophy of Science, Vol. 4 *(edited by Marx Wartofsky and Robert Cohen). He is currently working on a book using phenomenological thought to reconstruct an epistemological framework for the history and philosophy of science.*

[9]Daniel D. Williams, "The New Theological Situation," *Theology Today*, 24, No. 4 (January 1968), 462.

DANIEL DAY WILLIAMS

4

Changing
Concepts
of Nature

In this paper I will attempt a brief characterization of the classical Greek-Hellenistic concept of nature, and of the biblical-prophetic view. After summarizing the early modern view of the natural order, I will discuss three aspects of our situation today: (1) the new understanding of the concept of possibility and the openness of the future; (2) the politicizing of man's relationship to nature, with particular reference to ecological decisions; and (3) the representation of God's relation to nature in a temporalistic theism that reexamines immanence and transcendence, divine power and creaturely freedom.[1]

I. CLASSICAL AND BIBLICAL
VIEWS OF NATURE

Lucretius entitled his poetic vision of the world *De Rerum Natura (On the Nature of Things)*. Behind this usage of the term *natura* to designate the whole setting of man's life, including the swirl of atoms, the stars and the seasons, birth, decay, and death, there were centuries of Greek

---

[1]An earlier version of this essay was given at a conference of the Faith-Man-Nature group in November, 1969; see Glenn C. Stone, ed., *A New Ethic for a New Earth* (New York: Friendship Press, 1971).

48

philosophy, encompassing the pre-Socratics, Plato and Aristotle, and the atomists, all with their attempts to understand the moving forces and the intelligible structures of the world.

For Plato and Aristotle, nature, *physis*, was a panorama of processes, things in motion, growth and decay. The processes had their intelligible structures, and in their histories they worked out ends that were proper to them. Nature was the spatio-temporal scene of man's existence. Man shared in nature through his body, and through his mind he could explore nature's intelligibility. Yet for Plato and Aristotle there was a mystery, both in nature and in man, that involved an ultimate ground of nature that transcended the spatio-temporal order. For Plato it was the Form of the Good, the realm of pure Idea which was reflected in the earthly, bodily order. The human mind, Plato believed, could intuit this ultimate order and could move toward it. For Aristotle the goal we seek in our knowing was the final source of all motion, the pure thought, or pure intelligibility, which did not itself move but which moved all things just as the object of desire moves the lover.

We can speak of the whole order of things as "nature," or we can limit the term to the temporal processes and assert the transcendence of pure Idea or spirit over nature. Later Greek philosophies moved toward the concept of the supernatural origin of natural order. In Greek religion, even the gods had natures, and their lives and powers were bound up with events and possibilities in the natural world. These gods moved back and forth from the divine realm to earthly scenes.

Thus for the ancient world, nature could be experienced in bodily, mental, and spiritual modes. It could be enjoyed as the scene of satisfaction, or endured as the inflicter of wounds and death. Lucretius saw nature as the all-embracing tragic order of material processes that in the end produced man only to slay him, and he resigned himself to the enjoyment of the tragic vision. Other Greeks sought redemption from nature through a mystical and intellectual flight to its transcendent source, but this flight always began in nature, and its progress was dependent upon the discovery of nature's structures, her intelligibility, her reflection of an order of truth that lay at her base and never passed away. The Greeks saw nature partly under the overwhelming influence of mathematics and logic, and they gave to Western civilization this indispensable basis for the rise of modern science.

For the biblical view we turn to the prophets because they gave the most profound interpretation of the relation of God and nature. There was nothing in the Hebrew Bible that corresponded to the concept of nature as a system or order having its own life and structure as we have seen it in Greek thought. The prophets and psalmists knew the stars and the seasons, the life, passage, and death of the flowers of the field. They believed in a

Divine Orderer behind these regularities and dispensations. The Second Isaiah declared the ruling sovereign power of God:

It is he who sits above the circle of the earth,
And its inhabitants are like grasshoppers;
Who stretches out the heavens like a curtain
And spreads them like a tent to dwell in.... (Isa. 40:21–22)

We must be careful not to try to modernize the prophets. They thought within the world view of their times. They pictured God as immediately controlling and miraculously intervening in events. Modern conceptions of natural processes obeying discoverable laws and developing through infinite time were foreign to their view. Yet with all reservations, certain elements in the prophetic outlook are strikingly suggestive to us now. Nature, for all its dependability, we now know, is no fixed order with patterns that repeat themselves in endless cycles. As the prophets saw it, nature comes from the hands of God and serves his purposes. Therefore it is the scene of action, of passage, and it can be transformed. Everything in the created world is subject to the limitations of finitude, passage, and death; but everything by the same token can be seen as offering some potential new good to man as the dynamic life process goes on under God's purposive action.

For the prophets, nature bore the mystery of creation. It was not self-explanatory. Man's attempts to read its secret came up against the limits of human understanding. It was not a sheer riddle nor an arbitrary order, but its meaning was related to what God intended for man and for all his creatures. Therefore, there was always more to be known. The prophets' most radical idea was that nature as the society of created things was itself subject to God's redemptive action. God would remake and reorder it to fulfill his divine purpose. The biblical words are almost too familiar, and we forget their significance as the historical release from a fatalistic view of nature. "God turns a desert into pools of water, and a parched land into springs of water," said the psalmist (Ps. 107:33–36). The animal world was included in the transformation: "The wild beasts will honor me, and the jackals and the ostriches, for I give water in the wilderness." When we read the prophecy that "every valley shall be exalted and every mountain and hill made low," and that there will be a "highway in the desert," we may even feel in the light of modern highway systems that we have been overdoing our freedom to change the conditions of our natural life. In any case, nature for the prophetic outlook was the God-given environment for man's use. Jesus said, "Your heavenly father knows you have need of all these things."

Throughout the Bible the eschatological dimension is fundamental to the perspective in which the present world is seen. This present order is subject to the divine judgment. It is passing away. There are even traces in the Bible of a sense of the alienation of the whole creation from God: "The whole creation groaneth and travaileth in pain together until now," said Paul in Romans (chapter 7). Sometimes this eschatology involves a literal dissolution of the earth, as in II Peter: "The heavens will pass away with a loud noise, and the elements will be dissolved with fire, and the earth and the works that are upon it will be burned up" (3:10). It is worth noting that some eighteenth-century thinkers rejected this prediction of the universe's destruction on the ground that nature as described by eighteenth-century science was too intricate and beautiful to be destroyed.

For the early Christian view, and for most Christian theology through the centuries, whatever relative stability and meaning were assigned to nature as the spatio-temporal universe, it is always subordinate to God, its Creator, Judge, and Redeemer. God could intervene in special ways in the course of events. Miracles were signs of his power, and they might involve extraordinary displays of that power. Their meaning was not discoverable simply by observation; they pointed beyond themselves to the ultimate mystery of the divine.

II. MODERN CONCEPTS OF NATURE

Whitehead says that the rise of modern science owes much to the Christian faith in the dependability of God, coupled with the view of God's freedom to create as he will. There is no way of deducing the order of nature from purely a priori considerations. Man must observe and discover the order in the facts. Whitehead also assigns an important place to the theologians' dialectical skill that rested upon a faith in the intelligibility of the divine order once its premises have been given.[2]

The movement from classical Christian theology to the rise of the modern concept of nature is a complex history that has not been sufficiently studied. Attention would have to be given to the medieval appropriation of Platonism by way of Augustine, and the appropriation of Aristotle directly, and by way of the Arabians. The rise of modern science is related to this philosophical-theological development.

The eighteenth-century system of nature based upon Newton's achievement, which was the climax of centuries of scientific progress, gives the picture of nature as a mathematical-mechanical system, intelligible to reason.

[2]Alfred North Whitehead, *Science and the Modern World*, (New York: The Macmillan Company, 1925), Chapter 1.

Nature and Nature's laws lay hid in night
God said, "Let Newton be," and there was light!

Deism produced several types of adjustment of the belief in God to this new picture of nature. Newton himself defended the main features of the traditional theism, but when it came to finding a specific function for God after his creation of the world, he could only surmise that God brought order back into the machine when it got too far toward disorder, and that he kept the stars from collapsing in outer space.

Man's body is within nature. The tension between a mechanical view of nature in which the human body is as determined as anything else and the belief in human freedom comes to its climax in Hume and Kant, and much of modern philosophy has been an attempt to find some place for man's freedom in a nature that determines his existence.

There is however another aspect of the transition to the contemporary period. It is the naturalization of man's self-understanding. This familiar story could be told around three names: Copernicus, Darwin, and Freud. Man is part of a natural order that has its own history, its powers and structures that operate in part to bring man forth and sustain his life but also go their own way. Man belongs to the evolutionary process, sharing his origin and his instincts with all of animal life, and yet displaying new powers including his capacity to inquire into nature. Freud brings man's high self-estimate to confrontation with his instinctual life, which remains operative largely beneath the level of consciousness.

This naturalization of man is not reductionist in all respects. Man still is unique in so far as he knows. He has powers of reason, self-direction, and creativity that give him hope for the reshaping of nature towards human ends. Many evolutionary philosophies from John Fiske to Teilhard de Chardin have an ultimate optimism about man's future.

This naturalization of man, however, has important implications for our present situation. By "present" I mean since the discovery of nuclear weapons and the emergence of such scientific, cultural, and ecological issues as have become prominent in the later twentieth century. My thesis is that all these past frameworks for interpreting nature, and man's place in nature under God, are undergoing the shock of a new situation with unprecedented elements. No traditional structure of theological or philosophical interpretation is now adequate.

III. THE CONCEPT OF POSSIBILITY

The first aspect of the new situation is that the concept of possibility has emerged as fundamental for understanding both man and nature. Possibility stretches beyond actuality, and it involves an element of indeterminism with respect to the future. That which is possible is relevant to actuality, but its relevance is that of an as yet unrealized achievement. The concept of potentiality as an ultimate metaphysical aspect of nature certainly goes back to Aristotle. In the course of Western thought, it tended to be eliminated from the concept of nature by various determinisms, both theological and philosophical. In theological determinism every event is foreseen by God and willed by him. Therefore what seems to us like "possibility" is for God simply the not yet actualized conclusion that is already known to him. Philosophical determinism has sometimes drawn its assumptions from a view of scientific laws as eternally fixed, or from other philosophical considerations. Immanuel Kant thought that theoretical reason could not achieve a view of nature that allowed genuine freedom, and that the scientific view of the world required an absolute determinism; hence he had to "restrict science to make room for faith," and this meant moral faith in the significance of human choices.

In the twentieth century, however, there has been a sharp change of perspectives on the question of freedom. In the evolutionary philosophies and in modern physics, the concept of possibility, with an element of openness in the exact course of nature, appears genuinely acceptable if not required. It is true that the quantum theory and relativity physics do not prove we have the kind of freedom we mean when we speak of human freedom. But it is no longer intellectually defensible to reduce all human choices to the result of previously determined physical events. As Whitehead once remarked, "What is the sense of talking about a mechanical explanation when you don't know what you mean by mechanics?"

The philosophies of nature in our time do not view nature as a fixed system, but rather as a structure of potencies and processes that exhibit themselves in a creative activity, with the future in some measure genuinely open to new types of adjustment of life to its environment because the environment itself is plastic and unfinished.[3]

The philosopher Ernst Bloch has had a wide influence on contemporary views of history, and especially on the theology of hope. Bloch goes back in part to Aristotle's view of nature as embodying potencies for future realization. Bloch combines this with a humanistic philosophy of man as the bearer of freedom to create his own future. I call attention to a few sentences from one of Bloch's addresses to indicate the change in perspective on the future that this doctrine of nature as the bearer of "possibilities" involves.

> I presuppose that the world is open, that objectively real possibility exists in it and not merely determined necessity, not merely mechanical determinism. . . .

[3]Alfred North Whitehead, *Process and Reality* (New York: The Macmillan Company, 1929).

Openness toward the future is a large category which is handled perfunctorily. One must proceed beyond the horizon into that difficult degree of reality not of Being-Present (*Vorhanden-Sein*), nor of Being-in-Process (*Im Prozess-Sein*), but of Not-Yet-Being (*Noch-nicht-Sein*), into the sphere of the *Novum*, of the mediation of the deed, of fear and hope.

One must view the world as a task, as a model, *as an analysis of sample which is not at hand*. Science is necessary for this, a speculative, metaphysical science which understands the sky, which understands building up into the sky, the whole world is built up into the sky—indeed, a science which not only understands the blue of the sky but even its ultraviolet; and this with the knowledge that the presence which is usually called reality is surrounded by a tremendously greater ocean of objectively real possibility. Possibility is not hocus-pocus. It is an exactly definable concept; namely, partial conditionality. The world is not yet completely determined, it is still somewhat open: like tomorrow's weather.[4]

We note that Bloch's poetic language expresses a new sense of man's responsibility for the future and of hope for his fulfillment in that future.

Certainly to assert real possibility in the future offers no guarantee that the future will be the fulfillment of man's good. Bloch himself is aware of this. There is always the horizon beyond which we cannot see. The possibilities that the future holds may involve great evil as well as good. Although Bloch and many revolutionary philosophers seem to lean toward a kind of utopianism, the sober consideration of man's situation would seem to lead more reasonably to a view of the ambiguities of possibility as we look toward the future.

We see, as one alternative, the great promise of technological control over the environment, the possibility of food production adequate to support a very much larger population, and the release of human creativity through discovery of the conditions of a humane education. At the same time, we are aware of the threat of a population explosion that may get out of hand before society can provide the necessities of life for all, a threat of atomic and bacteriological warfare, and the possible dehumanization involved in the machine culture created by technological progress. The breaking of the genetic code is a good example of the ambiguity of man's achievements. It gives new dimensions to our thoughts on human possibilities. Man may direct his future growth by selecting the human material that he will encourage. Yet the uses to which such control might be put certainly have many sinister implications. Who is to decide what kinds of human beings are contributory to the real human good? What restrictions could be placed on such power of control?

[4]Ernst Bloch, "Man as Possibility," *Cross Currents*, 18, No. 3 (Summer 1968), 280–81.

The present situation does appear to give to man a dimension of power that he has never had before. Man is in the process of deciding what shape his future will take—within limits, at least, this seems to be the situation. Human action now, both individual and collective, bears the weight of responsibility for fulfilling, protecting, or destroying the rare and precious enterprise of human evolution on this planet. It is thus the exploration of the possibilities of nature, rather than the reading of assured directives in her, that gives the shape of both risk and hope to present human thinking about the future.

IV. THE POLITICIZING OF MAN'S RELATION TO NATURE

A second consequence of the new understanding is the politicizing of man's relationship to nature. What nature is, and how man can order his life within it—these are the issues that now have to be resolved within the political order. By "political" I mean the structures of decision-making power that involve the community as a whole. If it seems strange to speak of man's relationship to nature as political, this only measures the radical character of the new situation. There are three dimensions of this political aspect of ecology that we can explore.

The first is the obvious fact that the quality of human life and the possibility of human survival involve political solutions to problems of man's use of the environment. We need not multiply examples: preservation of wilderness and animal species, the expense of overcoming water and air pollution, the choice between spending billions getting men to Mars as against getting masses of city dwellers to work and back home in some decency and comfort—these are all issues of taxation, community control of resources, and decisions as to what needs to be done. Few areas of the common life today do not directly involve some political power and planning.

The second point is that the community as a whole is now having to make value-judgments about the environment and the use of nature. The political issues are also philosophical and ethical. Our experiences of one another, of the city and the countryside, and of seeking a fulfilled human life in nature are now bound up with political action. Consider our experience of space. The feeling of being crowded now enters into the quality of life. And the question of the use of space, including that of the "great out-of-doors" as we used to call it, is bound up with public policy, as anyone who has recently tried to stop or camp in national parks knows too well. Space itself is valuable. And what kinds of space do we need? Consider the wilderness issue. Why does man need to preserve the wilderness?

What are the relative values of keeping stretches of wilderness to be explored by a few hardy folk, as opposed to opening up the area with highways, lodging, and other services for many people and thereby losing the quality of wilderness? Such issues involve some of the subtlest questions about man and his needs that have ever been considered, and yet they are having to be answered by the makers of public policy.

Furthermore, the question of what is to be preserved and enjoyed in the environment is closely related to another question: "*Who* shall enjoy *what?*" Thus the issue of justice arises in all major ecological issues. For example, clean air seems to be an absolute value for all; but what determines where people must live and work has much to do with determining what kind of air they breathe. Access to a healthy, recreative environment is an economic issue, and it involves critical problems of justice that only the political community has the power to resolve.

Nature, then, is no longer simply a spectacle to be observed, but an assemblage of potencies, opportunities, and threats, all of which we perceive in relation to our human predicament. Our very physical perceptions and sensibilities are now being modified by the kind of interaction we experience with the environment. For instance, no one can look at the moon today and see it exactly as he did before man landed there. This is partly because we have seen pictures that have increased our awareness of what the moon is. The pictures of the earth taken from the perspective of the spaceships have also given us new angles of vision of the earth. It is interesting that this "earth-picture" has become a symbol for man's new situation. It has altered his self-image. In addition, the moon poses economic, political, and military questions. It has become a goal, or prize, and the nations are competing for its use for scientific and military purposes.

The third level of the politicizing of our relationship to nature has to do with the kind of expectation we have in history. Can man achieve a community of peace, productivity, and the release of his creative powers? If we are to avoid disaster, the movement of human life must be toward a *polis* of humanity. We cannot expect Kenya to preserve its marvelous richness of animal wildlife unless the international community is willing to share the financial cost. We cannot deal with the population explosion in some countries and not in others. Control of the drug traffic is an international problem. The development of food production requires the cooperation of governments, business, and science on a worldwide scale. World order under law is the only final alternative to suicidal warfare. We are led back to the profundity of the biblical view of history and the hope for the Kingdom of God as *a society of all* under God. A relevant Christian faith must bring this social hope into relationship with the present problems of collective life.

We are seeing, then, the passing of the concept that nature is a fixed setting for man's life, to be accepted with natural piety and contemplated in esthetic vision. Perhaps one could still stand serenely with Lucretius and recount in exquisite poetry the slow self-strangulation of the human race, but it somehow seems irresponsible. Francis Bacon in his day hailed the new scientific method as promising to render men the lords and possessors of nature. However, the results have been more ambiguous. Nature is not just what man makes of it; it is a field of as yet undetermined possibilities both for fulfillment and for destruction. We are, therefore, modifying, not discarding, the Greek vision of nature as an intelligible realm of potencies.

But in a way we seem closer today to the prophetic perspective. Nature and man are bound together in a fateful history where the responsibility of man for his life and for his world meets the demands of a new order in which a basic justice is required. Unless man responds to that demand, destruction is certain.

We see how the biblical images for interpreting the course and goal of history take on new meaning. Is there a guiding image for understanding man's adventure in history? There is the Adamic story with God's commission to man to establish "dominion" over the garden in which his life is set. "Dominion" is a political word. Indeed, some recent critics have said that Christianity is to blame for our ecological plight because this offer of dominion was taken as license for the exploitation of nature. Such a view is surely a great distortion of the biblical outlook. Actually what we have to do is to achieve a responsible dominion, and that must be exercised through the structures of power in the political communities.

The biblical story of the search for the promised land, following the release from slavery and the subsequent wandering in the wilderness where the community finds its law and its hope, offers a pattern of understanding of the meaning of history. Man finds himself a stranger in a nature that is part wilderness, and he seeks its transformation into a land where he can dwell in peace and decency. But the historical literalness of the hope of the promised land must be qualified by the insight into the transcendence of the Kingdom over specifiable earthly hopes. Paul's word, "It doth not yet appear what we shall be," keeps a proper restraint about historical predictions. The biblical hope is still a social and collective one. It is the hope for a new heaven and a new earth in which righteousness reigns, that is to say, a community bound together in charity and justice. In the Book of Revelation, the apocalyptic vision of the end suddenly turns a hopeful light on the history of the nations.

And the city has no need of sun or moon to shine upon it,
for the glory of God is its light,

and its lamp is the Lamb.
By its light shall the nations walk;
and the kings of the earth
shall bring their glory into it. (Rev. 21:23–24)

The biblical eschatology thus keeps the political dimension in its ultimate hope, but without demanding a political utopia in history.

V.   A NEW VIEW OF
GOD'S RELATION TO NATURE

We come finally to the implications of the new ecological situation for our ideas of God. Much contemporary theology has been engaged explicitly or implicitly, I suggest, in bringing this new openness of historical possibility into the theological outlook. Past forms of absolute determinism are being rejected. The process theologians following Whitehead have gone the furthest in asserting a dimension of potentiality in the divine nature itself. If God is related to a world of real possibilities, then God himself must be moving into a future that is in some measure open, even for him. Human decisions make a difference. They shape the future situation which God deals with. Limits are set by God's power and structure; but he responds to the real freedom of his creatures.

We must acknowledge that in modern theology there is a development that moves within the prophetic perspective but modifies it in the direction of the "naturalization" of the concept of God. John Calvin says in his *Institutes* that the expression "nature is God" may be used in a pious sense by a pious mind, "though strictly speaking we should speak of nature as an order prescribed by God so that we do not confound the Deity with his inferior works."[5] Christian theology, despite its supernaturalist heritage from the Hellenistic period, has never thought of God as completely separated from the natural scene of human life, or as so transcendent that he has no immediate commerce with earth and bodies and minds in space and time. But the relationship of God to the world in its processes, laws, and development has always been a problem for traditional theology, and it is critical for theology today.

Our modern experience of nature leads many theologians to affirm more emphatically the divine immanence in the world. God is not another name for evolution, or nature, or process, but he is the creative spirit and the ultimate order that makes process possible and order intelligible. If the process and the struggle in life are really significant, then God must

[5]John Calvin, *Institutes of the Christian Religion*, Book I, Chap. V, Section v.

be involved. It must make a difference to him what happens in nature. History is the field of the working of God's creative spirit through an unfinished, moving world. Natural laws are the relatively stable forms of process that are exhibited in particular cosmic epochs.

Such a radical view of the divine immanence marks a qualification of traditional doctrines of God's absolute transcendence over time and becoming; but it can retain the vision of God's transcendent reality. God is not simply one power among many. He is the ultimate and eternal reality upon whom all things depend for their existence and their value. What the new theism asserts is that if God is in actual relation to this world, he must participate in the becoming, the creativity, the real risk and adventure of being.

God's transcendence over the world is manifest in three aspects of his being. First, he is the power of being itself. It is God alone who has the power to determine that a world shall exist, to sustain it in being, and to interact with the whole of it. This is a supreme and incomparable power, but it is not the power traditionally ascribed to an absolutely omnipotent God. Instead, God gives the world its freedom to be a real world. The creatures add the novelty and decision of their own actuality to the stream of creativity. Unless the creatures have freedom to make some difference in the course of events, natural history and human history are but play acting. It would be all the same whatever happens or whatever men decide. But God's power is the supreme power to make existence possible for the creatures, and for them to have limited freedom to shape their own being.

God's transcendence is manifest also in relation to time, for he alone is unchanging and everlasting. What is distinctive in the new theism is that God as both temporal and eternal bears within himself the whole realm of possibility, which is the abstract structure of all actual events. Either there are real possibilities that lie before God as he and the creatures move into the future, or time is an illusion and history is meaningless. God transcends all time because he has neither beginning nor end; but within his everlastingness there is temporality as new acts of creation, new actions of the creatures, and new responses of God to the course of his world are made.

Finally, God's goodness transcends all finite values in two ways. First, God bears within himself the order of all possible good. There are real evils in the world. These are evil for God too, but they are the result of the risk of freedom for all creatures. Whatever possibilities of good there are for any creature and for any world depend upon God's being and his constituting the structure of all possible value. God's goodness is transcendent not only in its completeness of possibility but also in the integrity of the divine aim. God envisages a whole society of being, fulfilled in a creative harmony. This is not a plan or blueprint, but an ultimate ideal that is relevant to every concrete situation. Our finite visions of the good are broken and limited, and our commitment wavers, is perverted, and fails. But God's goodness is the unwavering guidance of the whole creation toward the fulfillments that are possible for each in the great community of all. His goodness is that of an unrelenting, unswerving, and wholly responsive aim toward the best for every creature in relation to all. God thus does not aim simply at his own good. He aims at the good of the whole creation, and that includes every part of the natural order, every living thing, and every beauty and power of existence.

I have stated this brief outline of a cosmic theism to show how God's relationship to nature can be conceived so as to do justice to the emerging new concept of nature and man's place in it. My interpretation of this theism is a version of the process philosophies of Alfred North Whitehead and Charles Hartshorne. The central ideas that it expresses, however, are not limited to one school of metaphysics, but are becoming the common property of those who are seeking a new philosophy of nature. Such a theism recovers many of the central themes of the biblical faith with its understanding of God's caring, suffering, redemptive purpose, and loving response to his world's needs.

Religious living in our time, if it is to be relevant to the ecological crisis, must involve our understanding of the obligations imposed upon us by our new situation in nature. Purely exploitative and purely submissive postures are equally dangerous. Religion is openness to the possibilities of life viewed in the light of a universal, constructive goodness at work in all things. That openness must be expressed in the ways man uses and explores the environment in which he lives.

I believe it is Henry Nelson Wieman in our time who has described with greatest clarity the form of religious devotion that responds to the creative possibilities in the interaction of God, man, and nature.[6] For Wieman, faith achieves its maturity in a commitment to the creative activity of God. In this activity the diverse experiences of life are welded into new integrations, new forms emerge, and new values and sensitivities are born. A response in the biblical spirit to man's situation in nature need not be blind worship of what is, nor sentimental affirmation of automatic progress. It need not retreat from the scientific attitude in exploring the possibilities of existence. It can be the hopeful, sacrificial determination to discover those conditions of man's relationship to his environment that release the great possibilities of his creative freedom. Our concepts of nature are being ploughed up, and we have to reconsider our human task

[6]Henry Nelson Wieman, *Man's Ultimate Commitment* (Carbondale: Southern Illinois University Press, 1958).

in the light of the new concepts. In the Christian outlook, God himself is
in the ploughing up and the remaking.

*DANIEL DAY WILLIAMS is Roosevelt Professor of
Systematic Theology at Union Theological Seminary in
New York. He was formerly on the faculties of Colorado
College and of Chicago Theological Seminary, and
was also a member of the Federated Theological Faculty
of the University of Chicago. His writings include* The
Andover Liberals, God's Grace and Man's Hope,
What Present-day Theologians Are Thinking, *and a
recent work,* The Spirit and the Forms of Love. *He has
been active in the Faith-Man-Nature group that has
been concerned with the relation of the Christian faith
to ecological problems.*

HUSTON SMITH

5

Tao Now

an ecological testament[1]

The rise of ecological concern in the West—swift, emphatic—is one
of the striking developments of our times.[2] My wife and I return from a
year abroad to find a sign over our kitchen disposal instructing us to "Save
all garbage for compost recycling—thanks a heap!" We open our mail and
find political candidates promising: "Not ecology rhetoric but ecology
action. . . . Stiffer sanctions against industrial pollutors. . . . The right of
private citizens to bring suit against violators." On my way to my office I
note that a storefront in Central Square has been converted into Ecology
Action; it is bustling. On reaching my office I find the top item on the
mountain of accumulated mail to be a house organ report of the 1970
Clean Air Car Race. My own institution's showing in the race appears to
have been spotty. Of the forty-three entered vehicles, M.I.T.'s steamer
didn't quite make it to the starting line, and its electric hybrid, plagued by

---

[1]It is now common knowledge that the Chinese character anglicized as "Tao" is pronounced "Dow." But for American students, especially radical ones, "Dow" has come
to denote Dow Chemical and, derivatively, napalm. Within this simple phoneme the
opposites have met.

[2]In progress, this statement formed the substance of the 1971 Mendenhall Lectures at
DePauw University, Gates Lectures at Grinnell College, Merrick Lectures at Ohio
Wesleyan University, and Distinguished Lecture Series at the University of Oregon.
I am indebted to audiences at those institutions for criticisms that helped to shape the
present formulation.

hard luck all the way, was barely maneuvering Oklahoma City as com-
competitors crossed the Cal Tech finishing line. Its turbine, on the other
hand, did well—a sure winner, being the only entry in its class.

What should we do? Our first impulse is to put on the brakes through
legislation. This is obviously needed: private citizens won't come to heel
without it any more than will the large pollutors. Legislation not only gets
results by virtue of the teeth in it; it also educes willingness. I resent pay-
ing 3¢ more for Amoco gas when the result is imperceptible, but I would
do so with a will if my act, joined by that of my fellow citizens, were party
to decreasing the lead content of my atmosphere appreciably. It's the difference between throwing my pennies away and buying clean air for that
little.

Still, legislation is limited. Pressure groups keep it from being fully
equitable, loopholes can be found, and there will always be a time lag
between the discovery of new ways to violate the environment and laws to
curb these ways. So while applying the brakes we need concomitantly to
press the accelerator. This means research: substantial allocation of public
and private monies to see how technology's usurpations and fallout can
leave our environment intact if not actually improved. The guiding principle here is the closed system. Instead of pouring industrial wastes and
sewage into our waterways and puffing smoke into the atmosphere, convert the pollutants mechanically and chemically into useful substances and
loop them back into the nutrient's cycle. "Pollutants are resources out of
place" is one of the heartening discoveries of our time, but the discovery
didn't fall into our laps. It required work—work that has only just begun.
So prohibiting legislation (injunctions) must be joined by enabling legislation for research, including research on how to keep our economy pros-
perous without built-in obsolescence. Luddite negativism is no answer.

I. THE NEED FOR A
NEW CONSCIOUSNESS

Prudential measures of this sort are important, but they need to be
undergirded by an altered stance toward nature itself. At least three ingre-
dients of our present posture could stand improvement. The first of these
is our presumption that nature has no claims, only uses. In antiquity each
tree, spring, grove, and hillock had its own *genius loci*, its guardian spirit.
Before one cut a tree, mined a mountain, or dammed a brook, it was
important to placate the spirit animating the domain in question. Moira
(fate), the Greek's earliest and ultimate posit, was at root a spatial concept, referring originally to the division of the world into distinct spheres
or provinces, each with its attendant rights and taboos. Nemesis grew out
of this notion. Originally she was a woodland goddess. As such she per-

sonified the woodland's sacred presence, a dangerous power not to be entered, not to be set foot on by persons who were not themselves sacred, sanctified, or ceremonially brought into a state in which contact with the mysterious power was no longer dangerous. When the profane did trespass, she became Avenging Anger and, as an extension of this, the goddess of retributive justice. Such views are far removed from technological man who, in Heidegger's phrase, has come to regard the world as a huge filling station.

Second, as nature is devoid of purpose, it is without compass or rudder. If left to its own devices, it cannot be trusted. This, too, represents a departure from earlier suppositions. At the start of Western philosophy, Thales announced that *physis*, the ultimate 'nature' of all things, is water and concomitantly is alive, 'has soul in it' in the same sense that there is a soul in the animal body. As organisms are remarkably resilient, homeostatic, and solicitous of their members, the thought that the world is alive inspires trust.

All in all, our emptying the cosmos of rights and life has positioned us toward it in a stance that is uncomfortable. For evidence I shall content myself with the balance of this single sentence: Heidegger's report that the world is that in the face of which one experiences anxiety, Beckett's key line in *Endgame* ("You're on earth, and there's no cure for that"), and Camus' reference in *The Myth of Sisyphus* to "this world to which I am opposed by my whole consciousness." Out of this discomfort grows the third aspect of our stance toward nature, which, in distinction to the foregoing two that are philosophical, is psychological and largely unconscious. Nature is that which we devour in our efforts to assuage our "dis-ease": its fruits to fill our emptiness, its distances to still our restlessness. Towards our planet's fare our civilization has come to exhibit the pathology of neurotic eating.

If our ecological difficulties stem in part from our outlook on nature, from whence might a different outlook derive? One possibility is that we could simply invent it, or conjure it up; but this possibility is more logical than feasible. To be more than fiction such a creation would have to derive from a myth maker the stature of which the world has seldom seen. More promising than an empty canvas as a starting point is our human past. In looking thereto we shall step back, as it were, in order to move forward, as when we retreat a little to take a running jump. No past perspective can fit present needs exactly, but there is the possibility that one might be updated. Moreover, the past has the advantage that in dealing with it we can be certain that we are dealing with more than fiction. Its contents grabbed man; at some stage of his development it connected with the wellsprings of his being. As we are members of the same species, we have a chance of finding in the outlooks of our ancestors elements that at some level of abstraction might speak to us also.

In scanning the past for suggestions it might seem sensible to begin with our own tradition, it being presumably more accessible. I do not discount this approach; other contributors to this volume ply it with results that are useful. It is not only to avoid duplication, however, that I propose myself to try a different tack. As our Western present has evolved from our Western past, that particular past may not be the best resource for advancing us beyond it. As it happens, my next section *will* be devoted to the West, but not in search of the clues we need. Rather the opposite: I want to show why, Western civilization having produced features in our world view that are giving us trouble, to counter these it may be helpful to look outside that civilization altogether.

II. THE WEST'S DISTANCING
FROM NATURE

The earliest respect in which the West showed signs of differentiating herself from the common stream of human development was in distancing herself from the given. Until she took this fateful step—stepping back, as it were, to place at arm's length and survey for the first time circumspectly and critically the milieu in which her life was set—mankind everywhere had lived under the spell of the cosmological myth. According to this myth, the given was God-given. Man's primal matrix was the living womb that sustained him. It existed to nurture him, not to be challenged, defied, or refashioned.

The Jews effected this distancing through Yahweh, a god who, unlike Baals and Astarte, did not evolve out of the natural processes of life and the soil but sprang into being through an extraordinary *un*natural occurrence: the improbable escape of a feeble, half-formed Hebrew tribe from the Egyptian juggernaut. Elsewhere in the Fertile Crescent, gods and nature fused. Not so in Yahweh; he was lord *of* events, deeds, history, and eventually of creation. He was forever commanding his people to do exceptional things, things that differed from the natural in the sense of the normal and conventional—what was already standard practice. "Get thee up. Go to the west to spy out the land. Go to the west, the fields are waiting."

What distanced the Greeks from the given is less clear, for by the time we first catch sight of them they seem already discernibly estranged. Hesiod's posit of a Golden Age was dropped in favor of Homer's less rosy view. The mythic ancestry of the Greeks is rife with crimes and perversities. Flagrant injustice abounds. Even the gods are party to it, impelling men to evil without purpose. And over it all broods Moira (fate), inexorable, master of men and gods, making puppets of both. When the Greeks looked outward onto their neighbors, the given that greeted them was no prettier than that in their own past, for their tiny land mass caused them to be ringed by foreigners who, partly in fact and even more in fear-filled fancy, were (in the word they coined) barbarians.

A small band set in a sea of 'given' that didn't comfort or appeal; what was the alternative? For the Jews it was Yahweh, his commanding and saving will. For the Greeks whose gods were accomplices in the given, this recourse wasn't open. If there was to be an alternative, it would have to come from man.

Reason was the logical candidate. Among man's faculties, mind has the largest purview: it can see backward through memory, forward through foresight, and to either side by entertaining its neighbors' interests even where it cannot feel these interests as its own. What better instrument for bringing order out of chaos?

It was all, as we say, so reasonable. But now we come to a key sector in our review. We must look at the notion of reason itself.

Intelligence is a generic human capacity, spread over the globe as far as we can tell in equal proportion; if Confucius or Kobo Daishi or Ramakrishna were not intelligent, then no one is intelligent and the word has no meaning. But intelligence can take many forms. We shall never understand our Western civilization in the sense of discerning the ways in which, and extent to which, it is a human option until we understand the peculiar *genre* of intelligence that has informed it. To denote this Western genre of intelligence I shall use the word 'reason'. How it developed out of the generic pool of human intelligence, delineating step by step its distinctive contours, is a story too involved for the telling here, even the parts we know. I shall content myself with indicating how the West's notion of reason derives from the Hebraic/Hellenic distancing from nature and doubles back to enlarge that distancing itself.

I back up for a running start. Mind advancing into increased self-consciousness is part of the meaning of civilization. By virtue of this advance, man confronts the given as if it were laid before him. As assessment is inevitable, some stance toward it is required. On reaching this choice-point, civilizations jumped differently. Asia retained a deep, unquestioning confidence in nature, appreciative of it, receptive to it. Had the Chinese and Indians not risen above the natural plane at all, they would not have spawned civilizations. The way in which they did transcend it, however, was by confirming it. They dignified it by affirming it consciously. By contrast the West oppositioned herself to nature in a stance that was reserved and critical. Its civilization receded progressively from the natural and instinctive and set itself up against them.

Consider the following contrast. On the eve of battle, Krishna is trying to help Arjuna, who is assailed by waves of pacifism, to discern his duty. It is axiomatic that his duty must be in accord with his nature. Plato assumes the same: intellectuals should rule, the courageous should guard and defend, and those of appetitive nature should produce. But how is one's nature to be ascertained? In India the answer is embedded in the given, specifically in the caste into which the individual is born. The possibility that an individual might be miscaste doesn't occur. Arjuna is a Kshatriya; Krishna's directive follows from that fact: "Therefore fight, O Bharata!" With Plato things are not this simple. Children will as a rule inherit their parents' natures and hence social positions, but this can't be counted on. In the *Gita*, "ought" follows from "is"; Given (what one should do) and given (one's social position) converge. In the *Republic*, not necessarily.

The difference is indicative. Asia's social philosophy has been more conservative throughout, and eminently natural in the sense of being grounded in strong instinctive drives. In the political sphere she never seriously questioned the natural extension of the tribal chief: autocratic monarchy. Power being a fact of social life, it is best to have it focused. A monarch effects this focus while monarchy as an institution extends it through time, across the generations. Closer to home, in the intimate sphere, China grounded social life in the family; India (with more ethnic and racial differences), in clusters of families or caste. All three forms keep within natural bonds; nowhere did Asia consider it man's function to interfere with existing social forms. Reform to her meant change in personnel—turning the rascals out—not institutional change. So ideology was left for the West where it flourished. Starting with Solon in Greece and the abolition of kingship in Rome, social and political movements were planned and carried out with increasing intensity in the name of theories, principles, and basic rights. How little Western man felt bound by natural ties, how much at liberty to replace them, is evident from the start. Plato doesn't hesitate to disrupt the family; reason can devise institutions that are better.

III. AN ESTRANGED AND ESTRANGING EPISTEMOLOGY

The West's compulsion to disengage from nature, to break from its womb and launch on an independent career, is not without effect, I am arguing, on her notion of reason—which notion, once formed, will influence everything that follows, the whole of Western culture. The effect was, in a word, to make division reason's basic operation. Intelligence deploying itself in the context of the West's distancing penchant was commissioned more for distinctions than for commonalities; it was by disposition better primed for analysis (the drawing of distinctions) than for intuition and synthesis (pulling together gestaltwise, at a glance and partly unconsciously, the multiple factors that converge in situations and require response). If Asia chose not to deploy intelligence primarily down reason's whole-splitting path, this was not entirely out of oblivion to the possibility. Partly it was because she sensed at some level the dangers that lurked.

From this foundational operation of reason, the drawing of distinctions, five other features emerge.

1. *Clarity.* Where distinctions are prized, clarity will be prized also. We are accustomed to the phrase "clear distinctions," but its words are really redundant. Insofar as it is genuine, every distinction is clear; to the degree that it is indistinct, the distinction itself is questionable—borderline cases are an embarrassment. When the father of modern philosophy, Descartes, built his methodology on clear and distinct ideas, the basic conjoint characteristic of Western reason surfaced to full consciousness.

2. *Generalization.* The distinctions of reason do not move toward indicating the individuality and uniqueness that each event possesses but rather in the opposite direction, toward isolating properties that members of the same class share in common. Ontologically reason strives for universals in objects, epistemologically for universals in thought, being interested (for example) in what treeness means for men generally and relatively uninterested in what a single tree might mean for me personally by virtue of the fact that I happen to love it. "From Socrates downwards," William James observed, "philosophers have vied with each other in scorn of the knowledge of the particular, and of adoration of that of the general." Far from being inevitable, he adds, this directionality is an "idol of the cave" and "hard to understand."

3. *Conceptualization.* Articulation and communicability go with this, for language and conceptual thought proceed together. When Socrates argues that every effective shoemaker will know his intended product and the use to which it is to be put, he speaks for human experience universally; but when he includes as integral to this knowledge the ability to describe these features of the product clearly, he speaks as architect of the specific version of knowledge that reason produces and the West promotes. This version is not the only kind of knowledge. There comes a point at which every craftsman reaches the limits of language and must say in effect, "I can't tell you what you are doing wrong, but let me have the chisel and watch how I shape that line," or "Let me have the keyboard and listen to how I take that passage." China with her "Tao that can be spoken is not the true Tao" and India's Upanishadic truth that can be comprehended only through living in the presence of a life through which

it actively shines (*Sad* = sit, *upani* = near to, under) hold closer to these tacit dimensions of knowing.

4. Implication. Western reason is interested in entailment, the if-then propensity, the impulse to see if from truth in one area anything follows about truths in areas that are adjacent and contiguous. This too derives from reason's proclivity to separate and divide, for unwinnowed experience is too complex to serve as the basis for inference. There are no laws of history, we say, giving evidence thereby of our realization that entailments hold only hypothetically or in restricted areas of actual experience. In demarcating these areas, separating reason establishes conditions wherein entailments become more readily evident.

5. Control. This too derives from reason's penchant for division; "divide and conquer" applies to the theoretical sphere no less than to the political. Life can be responded to as a whole, but it can be controlled only piecemeal: try to get it all out in front of you to order it about and you will be left with nowhere on which to stand. At least two distinctions are built into the very notion of control: the distinction between the way things are and the way they should be reordered, and the distinction between what is to be controlled and what will remain stable to provide footing for the operation.

In ways like these control requires distinctions, but distinctions need not in themselves awaken desires to control. They do so in reason because there they get implicated with the West's experience of the given as basically antipathetical and hence in need of monitoring. Several sentences rearranged from Chapter 5 of Herbert Marcuse's *Eros and Civilization* bring out the controlling coloration that reason early acquires, as succinctly as any I could compose to that precise end.

> When philosophy conceives the essence of being as Logos, it is already the Logos of domination—commanding, mastering, directing reason, to which man and nature are to be subjected. Nature (its own as well as that of the external world) were 'given' to the ego as something that had to be fought, conquered, and even violated. The struggle begins with the perpetual internal conquest of the 'lower' faculties of the individual: his sensuous and appetitive faculties. Their subjugation is, at least since Plato, regarded as a constitutive element of human reason. The struggle culminates in conquest of external nature which must be perpetually attacked, curbed, and exploited in order to yield to human needs. The ego experiences being as 'provocation' (Gaston Bachelard), as 'project' (J. P. Sartre); it experiences each existential condition as a restraint that has to be overcome, transformed into another one. Whatever the implications of the original Greek conception of Logos as the essence of being, since the

canonization of the Aristotelian logic, the term merges with the idea of ordering, classifying, mastering reason. And this idea of reason becomes increasingly antagonistic to those faculties and attitudes which are receptive rather than productive. The Logos shows forth as the logic of domination.

Civilizations are obviously too complex to evolve in any simple, linear fashion. They show few straight lines; usually it is a mélange of hens and eggs, circles, vicious and benign, and constant feedback. Thus the West's distancing of the given shapes its reason, while reason in turn pushes the given back still further, turning it into object. By "pushing back" I am thinking here primarily of psychological distance, but physical distance provides an accurate and influential analogy, for things must be held more or less at arm's length before they can be recognized as objects in their own right. The emergence of self-consciousness necessarily creates some gap between man and his world, but in the West the gap is greater.

The attitude that derives from taking the nonsubject to be fundamentally an object is, of course, objectivity. It involves, to begin with, a directionality, a mind that faces primarily outward. In alien territory or even in no man's land one needs to be wary; protracted introspection could divert attention from an environment that needs monitoring. So in contrast to Asia which focuses on the subject, the West concentrates on the outer side of the divide. It does so not only out of watchfulness and prudence but because the object, once on stage, actively invites attention. An immediate consequence is that disinterested thought becomes both natural and pertinent. Western epistemology develops along primarily realistic lines; buttressed by the Judeo-Christian doctrine of creation this encourages pure knowledge, not only applied. It also encourages philosophy to develop along lines distinct from theology and psychology, both of which, being soteriological, are subject-preoccupied. In Asia the three never divide.

Modern science and a penchant for the physical are only the most evident examples of the West's urge to posit objects everywhere, to confer on everything she encounters the form and existence of external entities. So when she turns from the outer world to inner experience—the object-oriented West always gets around to man *after* nature, whether the seminal period in question be Greek, Renaissance, or modern—the mind carries its objectivizing propensity with it. Thoughts come to be regarded as mental objects, universals as 'eternal objects', feelings as data. This doesn't require that these objects be physical in character; it's just that wherever the mind moves, it casts what it encounters into the mold of objectifiable phenomena. So literature and science vie with increasing vigor to unveil the variety and intricacies of the human soul—psychology and psychiatry, biography and autobiography, history, drama, and the novel, all get into the act. Asia shows little interest in this kind of phenomenology, contenting herself with a limited number of archetypical examples, for the most part ones that bear on edification. In the West the disclosures are valued for themselves, for they help fill in the map of existence, which, if the West had her way, would lie unrolled at her feet, complete. A mirror would make an even better image, for it would reflect everything precisely as it is, ideally distorted only in proportions, to render the small visible and the large comprehensible. This is the logical goal of the objectifying intellect, the final desideratum of its unceasing urge to confront reality as a totality of concrete, preferably picturable, objects.

What happens to truth when intelligence takes the form of reason with its separating bent and the world takes on the guise of object? At the onset of all civilizations, truth is interchangeable with reality: Whether we look at *satyam* in Sanskrit, *haaq* in Arabic, or *verus* in Latin, the matter is the same: all of these words denote what is real, genuine, and authentic on the one hand, and what is valid and accurate on the other. In Asia this generous denotation persists, but in the West it has shriveled; truth (and its opposite, falsity) are now taken by the West to be strictly predicable of statements only. Two simple steps lead to this conclusion. In the first step, the West's objectifying penchant depersonalizes truth. Traces of the earlier referent linger in phrases like "to thine own self be true," "true courage," "true to one's wife," and the New Testament reference to "doing the truth," but philosophy comes to dismiss these as metaphorical and not really legitimate—only propositions are *really* true or false. The remaining step is to withdraw truth from impersonal reality. As long as the Great Chain of Being was in place, reality admitted of degrees; so it made sense to speak of God as more real than man and of man as more real than arti-facts. Truth's accountability to such ontological gradations continues, too, as in our allusion to "true tones," or "true north." But since the West's objectivizing tendency pushed reality beyond the pale of value entirely, these statements too are taken to be bred of confusion if intended literally. Notions of degree have no place in reality. A state-of-affairs is a state-of-affairs; it either exists or it doesn't. How then can it be either true or false?

For a civilization to relegate truth to the realm of impersonal propo-sitions is to position itself toward the world in a special and far-reaching way. In the natural sciences this positioning does much good and no harm; elsewhere this is less clear. Gandhi could mobilize an entire people around *Satyagraha*, "truth-force," and through it liberate a nation. Our canons have no room for such a notion; to us it appears a pastiche, a conflation of intentions and dispositions that a clear mind will distinguish and lay out in patterned array. Thereby again our ties to the given are loosened and neurotic eating continues.

Objective knowledge, taken as a paradigm, points in the same direction. As with the notion that truth is impersonal, the notion that knowledge ideally is objective is unexceptionable in technology and the sciences; but when it is extended to knowledge of meanings and values, it produces unanticipated consequences, ones so important that they have provoked an entire movement to counter them. The concern of existentialism with such topics as dread, death, choice, and the self has not been out of interest in these subjects as self-contained; at bottom it has been because these topics, being intensely personal, provide natural entrées for challenging the claim of objectivity to be the only reliable route to knowledge. For objectivity pulls counter to selfhood. Selves are individual; as no two have the same genetic composition or are shaped by the same ontogenetic influences, so none ever beholds the world with eyes identical to another's. Objectivity seeks to remedy this perspectival "defect" by seeking knowledge that is valid for everyone. To maintain that such knowledge can do justice to selves in every important respect entails the view that their differences are not important; it is like holding that a single GI-clothing issue can suit all bodies. As individuality is too much a part of our constitution to be thus discounted, objective knowledge cannot be wholly satisfying. It holds, moreover, a specific danger: If extended unduly it leads, as Nietzsche saw, to nihilism. For if, per the objectivist ideal, we were to succeed in getting all our values out in front of us, completely visible to our conscious understanding, one decisive move would remain—to espouse them or to shrug and walk away.

IV.   THE TURN TO THE EAST

Nothing is gained by turning intelligence off, but sometimes it needs to be deconditioned. With this profoundly subversive intent I propose now to cut out of Western civilization completely, to prune back its impersonal truth, objective knowledge, and its view of reason as dividing and controlling, so that I can touch base with the common water table of mankind, the primeval outlook from which all civilizations evolved. This archaic outlook I have called the cosmological myth; it depicted nature, society, and self as fused in a more or less compact unity. Moreover, having worked our way back to this primordial base, I propose to veer sharply to the East. For although even archaic man has had thoughts that could help us if we could update them, there is an obstacle. We are civilized. China, I suggest, may help us across the gulf this poses. For China developed the cosmological myth, neither stagnating in it as did the tribes that remained primitive, nor veering from it as did we in the West. My hope is that in this our time of ecological need it may prove suggestive to see how the primordial philosophy out of which all civilizations evolved looks when it is updated, modulated by cultivated expression within the bosom of a full-fledged civilization.

China developed the cosmological myth by viewing the universe as an organic system of interdependent parts. This view disclosed the individual as being in the first place the recipient or heir to an endless flow of blessings issuing most noticeably from his parents but behind them from his ruler and from heaven and earth in their entirety. By virtue of these benefactions, the individual owes a debt of service to those from whom they issue. In particular he owes debts of filial piety to his parents and loyalty to his ruler. Where life is in balance these debts will be repaid spontaneously, motivated by the gratitude that the benefactions instinctively awaken in the recipient. Expressed metaphysically, the view led to the notion of the fundamental unity of all things in their essential aspects. The individual who seeks for his own true soul will discover it to be the same as the soul of heaven and earth and all things. The quest partakes of mysticism, but in East Asia, not a world-rejecting mysticism. Once the individual discovers his supreme identity, he is able to live in harmony with his social and natural environment.

To designate this complete divine ecology, the Chinese used the word Tao. What can we say of it?[3]

The first thing we must say is that it is impossible to describe it objectively, that is to say, in a way that will be publicly convincing. This is obvious when we think of the world's worth; if I were to claim I could persuade someone recently disillusioned in love or someone saddled with a deplorable self-image that life is a magnificent adventure, you would think me mad. Any objective description of the world would have to be value-free. But the world is not value-free; to assume that it is, is the ontological dead end into which we Westerners have been driven by our

---

[3]What I say of it here is what *I* shall be saying. This is not an historical study; if it were, the entire space could be devoured by the question of which Tao to describe—that of the Six Classics, of Confucianism, of Neo-Confucianism, of the Chinese Buddhism that caused Dwight Goddard to include the *Tao Teh Ching* in his *Buddhist Bible?* If the response is, "Not these, surely, but the Tao of the Taoists themselves," there is still the question of which Taoist: philosophical, mystical, or popular-religious? (See my chapter on the subject in *The Religions of Man.*) What follows is a composite that draws mainly on the *Tao Teh Ching* and Chuang Tzu, more on the former than the latter, but it follows their seminal intuitions as these saturate other strands in the Chinese fabric, notably Ch'an Buddhism. In addition, the statement undoubtedly contains emphases occasioned by the angle from which I am approaching the subject. I am looking for a concept that might speak to us in our ecological need. I find this concept in the Tao that emerges from my Chinese meditations; but if a reader wishes to object that it is difficult to match my depiction to a single concept, individual, or school in classical China, he may be right.

peculiar canons of knowing. Another way to indicate that the Tao eludes objective demonstration is to say that knower and known are correlative. We see what we are capable of seeing, know what we can know. But the Tao, according to one thoughtful soul, Dwight Goddard, "is the name given to perhaps the grandest conception the human mind has ever conceived." It would be puzzling, therefore, if it *were* in focus to casual, surface inspection.

The Tao cannot be objectively described, then, in the sense of being depicted in a way that is logically consistent and intuitively plausible to all. To assume the contrary would be to continue in the Western objectivist mistake. The only approaches to it are the way of letters and the way of life. The way of letters is the poet's way: by verbal wizzardry to trigger an astral projection of our moods and imaginings to another plane. The way of life is different. It requires long years of cultivation, for it requires altering not one's imagination but one's self; transforming one's sentiments, attitudes, and outlook until, a new perceptual instrument having been forged, a new world swings into view.

This world of the accomplished Taoist, of the man whose psychic integration has progressed to the point where not only are his inner forces harmonized but the sum of these are attuned to his enveloping surround —what is this world of the perfected Taoist like?

It is the Realm of the Great Infinite. Here too let us acknowledge that even the accomplished Taoist can have only the slightest sense of what this realm is really like. We approach it as men, with minds and senses that suffice for our needs but fall as far short in their capacity to discern reality's ultimate nature as an amoeba's intelligence founders before Einstein; if physicists like David Bohm and Phillip Morrison can suspect that the levels of size in the universe—transstellar, mega, macro, micro, subquantum—are infinite, a sage may be pardoned his hunch that its value-reaches are comparably beyond our ken. To be in any way manageable our question must be modified to read: What is the profoundest view of the Realm of the Great Infinite available to man?

1. It is a realm of relativity. Perhaps, as Kierkegaard put the matter, existence *is* a system—for God; for man, who is within it, system it can never be. Within it, all is perspectival. The flower, in front of the candle to me, is behind it to my wife. One stone is light compared to a second, heavy compared to a third. The pitch of a locomotive's whistle is constant for the engineer; to a bystander it falls. Nothing can be absolutely positioned, for we lack the absolute framework such positioning would require. If this is true of perception and thought, it must also hold of course for language. It being impossible to say everything at once, every statement is perforce partial; it is one-sided. But the world itself, being in us and around us, is never one-sided. All this holds, of course, for the present

statement. Naturally I shall try to make my account of the Tao as cogent as possible, for if I begin to fail glaringly, I shall myself lose interest as quickly as will you. Still, somewhere in my words there will be a flaw— that's a priori; somewhere in my depiction is a value counterpart of the surd Goedel spotted in mathematics: a point that contradicts something I say elsewhere or collides with a piece of your considered experience. We should not bemoan this buckle in our logic, for it keeps us moving, keeps us from settling down, insists on an extension in our horizons if it is to be smoothed out. If it doesn't show itself today, it will tomorrow.

2. It is a realm of interpenetration and interdependence. It is not one in a simple sense that excludes distinctions and could be visualized as the clear light of the void, a sky unflecked with clouds, or the sea without a wave. Distinctions abound, but the domains they establish cohere. "Heaven and Earth and I live together, and therein all things and I are one" (Chuang Tzu).

> Thirty spokes joined at the hub.
> From their non-being [i.e., the point at which their
>   distinctnesses disappear in the hub itself]
> Comes the function of the wheel (Lao Tzu).

Multiplicity is itself a unity. As nothing exists by itself, all things being in fact interdependent, no phenomenon can be understood by divorcing it from its surround. Indeed, it is the underlying unity that provides the possibility *for* distinctions. Thus even parts that appear discordant unite at some level to form a whole: "Tweedledum and Tweedledee/ *Agreed* to have a battle." Or like elderly chess players who, having done their utmost to vanquish each other, at game's end push back the board, light up cigarettes, and review the moves as friends. Being is organic. Peculiarities dissolve, parts fuse into other parts. Each individual melds into other individuals and through this melding makes its contribution, leaves its mark.

This complementary interpenetration is symbolized in many ways in China. One of the best-known ways is the *yin-yang*, a circle divided into black and white halves, not by a straight line but by one that meanders, leading white into black domain and allowing black to lap back into the white. Moreover, a white dot stakes its claim in the deepest recesses of black, while a black dot does likewise in the central citadel of the white. All things do indeed carry within themselves the seeds of their own antitheses. And the opposites are bonded; banded together by the encompassing circle that locks both black and white in inseparable embrace. On a two-dimensional surface, no symbol can rival the yang-yin in

depicting the Great Infinite's complementing interpenetration, but because it remains to the end two-dimensional, it needs supplementing. Our
two cats when they sleep lapped over one another are a three-dimensional
yin-yang, and indeed when they fight they form a four-dimensional one.
But man needs to feel the play of these forces in himself kinesthetically,
not just observe them in others. So the Chinese created *Tai Chi*, the Great
Polarity, a discipline that cuts right across our disparate categories of
calisthenics, dance, martial arts, and meditation. In lieu of a film strip I
insert here some notes I once jotted down at a Tai Chi class:

> Everything a little curved; nothing extended or pushed to the limit. Ex-
> pansive gestures (out and up) are yang, ingathering gestures (down and
> in) are yin. No side of the body exclusively one or the other. Yang dis-
> solves at once into yin, yin gathers strength to become yang. Down be-
> comes up, up down. All is lightness and freedom. As soon as it's done,
> stop; no sooner heavy than grows light. Strong, then immediately release.
> Energy reserved, highly volatile, capable of being deployed in any direc-
> tion, at any point. So finely balanced that a fly cannot alight nor feather
> be added.

Apocryphal like all such stories, yet making its point, is the account
of the great master, Yang Chien Ho. Birds were unable to take off from
his palm because as their feet pushed down to spring, his hand dropped
concomitantly. Drawing a cocoon thread is another image; if there is
no pressure the thread isn't drawn, but the instant there is too much
the thread snaps.

3. Viewed extrovertively, under the aspect of yang, the interrelated-
ness of existence shows forth as the Great Creativity. From a single
primordial atom the entire universe derives: galaxies, nebulae, island uni-
verses, pushing forward faster and faster. Potentiality explodes into actuality, infinitely. Every possibility must be exploited, each nook and cranny
filled. Thereby diversity is accomplished. When attention shifts from this
multiplicity to its relatedness, the Great Sympathy comes into view. As
sympathy, Tao synthesizes; as creativity it proliferates. The two movements
complement; creativity flows from one to all, sympathy from all to one.
Without sympathy multiplicity would be chaos, whereas without creativity
sympathy would lack province. They proceed together, hand in hand,
partners in the Tao's sublime ecology. Chuang Tzu's illustration, characteristically homey, is the centipede. At the points at which they touch the
earth its legs are a hundred or so, but on a higher level such orchestration!
It is through the many that the one enacts its versatility.

Perceived thus in the context of the Tao, nature to the Chinese was

no disenchanted causal mechanism floating on the foundation of nothing-
ness. It was undergirded by an eternal numinous reality from which life
proceeds and which inclines it towards harmony. Underlying the visible
—our phenomenal world, the "realm of the ten thousand things"—is something of immense importance that is invisible. The essential relation between the two is nonduality. Life's dependability, mingling with nature's,
betokens a hidden oneness in the bosom of the multiple, a total interdependence at the heart of the spheres. A rhythm falls upon the visible,
breaking it into day and night, summer and winter, male and female, but
these divisions are caught up and ordered in a superior integration that
resolves the tensions and reconciles the irreconcilable. Heaven and earth
agree. They are united in a hymn for a double choir, an antiphony on a
cosmic scale. It is a concentric vision, the vision of society set like a stone
in nature, and nature set similarly in the deep repose of eternity.

V. THE LADDER OF ASCENT

To experience reality as just described results in sensing a friendly
continuity between one's own life and the Tao, and a willingness to blend
with its ways. There comes also a shift toward *yes* and away from *no*
where the claims of the nonego are concerned and a consequent freedom
and elation as the boundaries of confining selfhood melt down. A gen-
eralized sense of life's enlargement and well-being commences. How to
get into this state—the question of method—lies outside the scope of this
paper, but I will note five stages through which the aspirant is said to
pass.[4]

1. He begins with the world as it appears to men generally, composed of discrete and apparently self-subsisting entities that are related
only in such ways as empirical observation discloses.

2. The second stage involves a dramatic awakening in which the
world's undifferentiated aspect is realized. This is the world known to
mystics and a good many artists. Individual selfhood vanishes; one becomes merged with the Great Self, Emptiness, or the Void.

3. But we live in the everyday world, the world of relativity and

[4]The first four steps are taken from the *Hua-yen* school, which, building on
Buddhism and hence indirectly on India's willingness to attempt to conceptualize
positions the Chinese would have left intuitive, articulated the doctrine of "perfect mutual unimpeded solution" more explicitly than did any other school in
East Asia. The fifth step is added by the Ch'an school.

separate things. So the next step is to realize that noumena and phenomena, the relative and absolute worlds of stages one and two respectively, are but two aspects of one reality. With feet planted in the absolute the aspirant is directed to look anew at the relative world that he previously took to be the only world. He must come to see that the phenomenal is in truth but the aspect under which the noumenon is perceived. Absolute and relative completely interpenetrate without obstruction or hindrance. They are one and the same thing. With this realization the aspirant discovers that everything in the world about him, every tree and rock, every hill and star, every bit of dust and dirt, as well as every insect, plant, and animal, himself included, are manifestations of the Tao and their movements are functionings of the Tao. Everything, just as it is, is in essence holy.

4. But more lies ahead. One must come to see that the things that have already come to be recognized as manifestations of the Tao together form one complete and total whole by means of harmonious and unobstructed penetration, interconvertibility, and identification with each other. Everything in the universe is realized to be constantly and continuously, freely and harmoniously interpenetrating, interconverting itself with every other thing. A favorite symbol here is Indra's net, each intersection of which lodges a jewel that reflects all the other jewels in the net together with the reflections each of them contained. The problem with this symbol is the same as that which we encountered in connection with the yin-yang a net, too, is static, whereas the point is to grasp dynamically the Tao whose nature is always to move on. This requires that the grasper himself be forever in the mood of moving, this being the character of life itself. Taoist terms are, for the most part, dynamic rather than static, terms like 'entering-into' and 'being-taken-in', or 'taking-in', 'embracing-and-pervading', and 'simultaneous-unimpeded-diffusion'.

5. Finally, and characteristically Chinese, there is 'the return to the natural'. Having come to recognize every element in the world and every act as holy and indispensable to the total universe, as this realization deepens and grows increasingly profound, it is no longer necessary to think explicitly about such things. It is enough for things to be affirmed in their own right; each moment can be responded to naturally and spontaneously as sufficient in itself. It is in this culminating state that one realizes with Master Nansen that "the everyday mind is Tao." Trudging through the snow a master and disciple were surprised by a rabbit that sprang out of nowhere and bounded across their path. "What would you say of that?" the master asked. "It was like a god!" the disciple answered. As the master seemed unimpressed with the answer, the disciple returned the question: "Well, what would you say it was?" "It was a rabbit!"

VI. QUIETISM:
THE TEST OF THE THEORY

Every position has its problematic, a shoal that, navigated or foundered upon, determines whether the system stands or falls. For Taoism the danger is quietism, the reading of its pivotal *wu wei* (no action) doctrine as admonishing us to do as little as possible or in any case nothing contrary to natural impulse. If everything is an aspect of Tao and thereby holy exactly as it is, why change it? Or to put the question another way: Since, although the Tao's parts are always in flux, its balance of forces is constant, why try to shift its parts from one place to another?

The path that winds past this precipice is a narrow one, and time and again China fell off it. Indeed, one can read the entire history of philosophical Taoism, as well as Buddhism in its Taoist variant (Ch'an), as one long struggle to keep from reading Chuang Tzu's "Do nothing, and everything will be done" as counselling sloth and rationalizing privilege. What other reading is possible? If the answer is "none," the jig's up. If Taoism ends up admonishing us to lounge around while tsetse flies bite us, to sink back in our professional settees, handsomely upholstered by endowments amassed from exhorbitant rents in ghetto slums; if Taoism suggests that we rest on our oars while our nation mashes peasant countrysides in Southeast Asia, the sooner it is forgotten the better.

The doctrine cannot be stated to preclude such misreading, but the misreading itself can, with care, be avoided. Helpful to doing so is the realization that Taoist assertions are made from the far side of the self/other divide, being in this respect the Orient's equivalent of "Love God and do what you please." *Wu wei* can be read unequivocally only after one has attained Tao-identification. At that point one will continue to act —the Tao, we recall, is never static; to be in it is to be always in the mood of moving—but the far shore attained, one need do nothing save what comes naturally, for what needs doing will claim one's will directly. Unobscured by attachment to ones own perquisites, the suffering of the dispossessed will draw one spontaneously to their side. Until that point is reached there must be labors that are not wholly spontaneous as we try to act our way into right thinking while concomitantly thinking our way into right action.

The Tao is not unilateral yin. Sensing that even in China when the Tao hits man's mind it tends to enter a yang phase, Taoism sought to redress the balance, but the balance itself was its true concern. "Now yin, now yang: that is the Tao" (*The Great Commentary*). The formulation is exact; countering man's disposition to put yang first, Taoism throws its ounces on the side of yin, but to recover the original wholeness. That emphasis is what we need as well. "Heroic materialism" is the phrase Kenneth Clark used on the concluding program of his *Civilization* series to characterize our Western achievement; pointing to the Manhattan skyline he noted that it had been thrown up in a century, about a third of the time it took the Middle Ages to build a cathedral. With an impunity Asia would not have believed possible, we have indulged ourselves in a yang trip the likes of which was never before essayed. And we are still here; we haven't capsized. But if we have arrived at a point where taste as well as prudence counsels a redressing, the Tao stands waiting in the wings with "now yin" as its first suggestion. It doesn't ask us to dismantle our machines; civilization needn't be de-yanged. Its call is simply to open the sluice gates of our Great Sympathy to let it catch up with our Great Creativity. The virtues of mastery and control we have developed to near perfection, but life can't proceed on their terms alone.

To enter a friendship, to say nothing of marriage, with an eye to control is to sully the relationship from the start. Complementing the capacity to control is the capacity to surrender—to others in love and friendship, to duty in conscience, to life itself in some sustaining way. The same holds for possessions and complexity; we know well the rewards that they can bestow, while knowing less well the complementing rewards that derive from simplicity. When a Western musicologist was seeking help in deciphering the score of certain Tibetan chants, he was informed by the Karmapa that they "could only be understood by a perfect being, there being so much to hear in a single note." And fronting Eiheiji is Half-Dipper bridge, so-called because whenever Dogen dipped water from the river he used only half a dipperful, returning the rest to the river. Such sayings and behavior are difficult for us to understand; they tend to be beyond our comprehension. But if we were to feel the beauty of the river and a oneness with the water, might we not feel its claims on us and do as Dogen did? It is our own true nature, our natural 'uncarved block' as the Taoist would say, to do so.

Simplicity and surrender can appear as high-ranking values only in a world one trusts and to which one feels at deepest level attuned. If the Taoist approach to nature was not based on reasoned strategy and well-planned attack, it was because such stratagems appeared unneeded. Western civilization has tended to regard the world either as mystery to be entered through religious initiation or as antagonist to be opposed with technological adroitness or stoical courage. Greek tragedy and philosophy set the tone for this; modern science and technology have amplified it a hundredfold. Western man has been at heart Promethian; therein lie both his greatness and his absurdity. Taoism does not try to beat or cajole the universe or the gods; it tries to join them. The Western stoic tries this tack too, but from the premise of antagonistic wills to be reconciled by obedience or overcome by dogged refusal. To Asia the problem is a matter of ignorance and enlightenment. If seventeenth-to-nineteenth-century science saw the world as mechanism and twentieth-century science is seeing it (with its holism, reciprocity, and growth) as resembling more an organism, is it possible that the twenty-first century will see it as —what? Is the savingly indefinite word "spirit" appropriate? "If I could say impersonal person, it would be that" (Sokei-an).

> There is a being, wonderful, perfect;
> It existed before heaven and earth.
> How quiet it is!
> How spiritual it is!
> It stands alone and it does not change.
> It moves around and around, but does not on this account
>   suffer.
> All life comes from it.
> It wraps everything with its love as in a garment, and yet it
>   claims no honor, it does not demand to be Lord.
> I do not know its name, and so I call it Tao, the Way, and
>   I rejoice in its power.[5]

HUSTON SMITH is Professor of Philosophy at the Massachusetts Institute of Technology. Born and raised in China, he has written The Religions of Man, Condemned to Meaning, *and* The Purposes of Higher Education, *and he is editor and coauthor of* The Search for America. *Bearing on his essay for the present volume is his chapter "Transcendence in Traditional China" in James Liu and Wei-ming Tu's anthology* Traditional China.

[5]Adapted from K. L. Reichelt's translation of the Twenty-fifth Chapter of the *Tao Teh Ching*, in his *Meditation and Piety in the Far East* (New York: Harper & Row, Publishers, 1954), p. 41.

WILLIAM G. POLLARD

6

The Uniqueness

of

the Earth

One of the most significant general results of our space program has been the new perspective on our Earth achieved for all mankind with the magnificent color pictures of the planet brought back from the Apollo missions. The amazing beauty of the Earth with its swirling white cloud cover and the sparkling azure of her oceans is breathtaking. From out in space where the Earth can be seen as one among many astronomical objects, no other planet has anything to compare with her beauty.

The Earth has an incredibly long history, and her present adornment of atmosphere, hydrosphere, and biosphere is the achievement of that history. It was made possible by a remarkable and delicate combination of circumstances that when fully appreciated suggests a largely unrecognized uniqueness for the Earth. This can be best appreciated by considering the history of the Earth in parallel with the contrasting histories of the other planets in the solar system and of the sun itself. For this purpose a number of other less well known missions of the United States and Soviet space programs have provided much new and relevant information. With this information combined with knowledge derived from other sources, a fairly reliable general account of the history of the solar system can now be given.

I. THE EARTH AMONG THE PLANETS

The sun and planets were formed 4.6 billion years ago in the collapse of a great cloud of gas and dust falling in on itself under its own gravity. The gases were mainly hydrogen and helium with the less abundant carbon, nitrogen, and oxygen present as methane (CH_4), ammonia (NH_3), and water (H_2O). Floating in this gas was a relatively small amount of dust of silicates and metals, mostly iron. The heavy elements from iron through uranium in this cloud had been freshly synthesized 100 or 200 millions of years earlier in a vast explosion of a previous star that became a supernova.

Most of this cloud condensed into a large central body that became the sun. A few tenths of a percent of it, however, were thrown out by centrifugal force in the rotating collapsing mass into a great platter in the plane of the sun's equator like the rings of Saturn. In the meantime the center of the condensing mass became hotter and hotter as the gas was more and more compressed. Soon the temperature at the center of the sun reached the hydrogen bomb ignition temperature of several million degrees centrigrade, and the hydrogen in the central core ignited explosively. This explosion has been going on ever since in the sun's central core for the last 4.5 billion years. Elsewhere in the universe, before and since, other interstellar gas clouds have been undergoing gravitational collapse in the same way and producing stars. Our own galaxy contains over 100 billion of them, and new ones are being formed all the time.

The young sun was quite active, producing great solar flares and an intense solar wind. In the first 100 million years this swept much of the hydrogen and helium out of the space near the sun well beyond the present orbit of Mars. The heavier materials in the meantime condensed into growing chunks of stone and iron with a good deal of ice and some entrapped ammonia and methane in them. These in turn amassed in growing bodies that became the lesser planets: Mercury, Venus, Earth, Moon, Mars, and the Asteroids (prevented from consolidating into a planet by the powerful gravity of nearby Jupiter). Farther out, the very cold hydrogen and helium were gathered under their own gravity and condensed into the major planets: Jupiter, Saturn, Uranus, and Neptune—low density bodies very different from the inner planets. Jupiter and Saturn may have central cores of solid helium surrounded by thick mantles of metallic hydrogen and outer atmospheres of hydrogen, ammonia, and methane.

At first all of these inner planets, including the Earth, must have been much alike—bare rocky bodies pockmarked with craters during their growth by the impact of great chunks of rock. The melting of this rock on impact released the entrapped water, ammonia, and methane, so that as the planets grew this atmosphere grew with them. In all of them, radioactive materials—mainly uranium, thorium, and potassium generated in the ancestral supernova—steadily generated heat deep in their interiors. Possibly the Earth and Venus collected more iron, uranium, and other metals than did the Moon and Mars, and so experienced greater internal heating. In time this internal heat melted the rock, and the rising pressure released it in volcanoes with great lava flows and additional quantities of steam, methane, and ammonia.

Only the Earth was at just the right distance from the sun for the released steam to condense as rain and collect over the surface in rivers, lakes, and eventually oceans. On Venus and Mercury the temperature was always too high for this, and the steam remained in their atmospheres as water vapor. On Mars it came down as snow and collected as ice. Only occasionally in brief warm periods would there have been liquid water on Mars such as one sees here on the Greenland ice cap. For the first several billion years the Moon may well have been a separate planet in an orbit around the sun near the Earth's orbit.

There are two important and somewhat related points to be made about the hydrogen-containing compounds—methane, ammonia, and water—in the early history of all these planets. At the top of their atmospheres the intense ultraviolet light from the sun continually knocked hydrogen atoms out of all of these molecules. The very fast moving hydrogen atoms when moving directly away from the planet would occasionally have enough velocity to escape from it completely. This was very much the case with the Moon for which the escape velocity is only 1.5 miles per second. For Mercury and Mars it is a little over 3 miles per second, but the much higher temperature of the former would produce a much more rapid escape of hydrogen from it. For Venus and the Earth the escape velocity is about 7 miles per second, so the hydrogen would escape much more slowly.

Ultimately when all the hydrogen is gone, the oxygen left behind from the water combines with the carbon left behind from the methane to form carbon dioxide. The oxygen also combines with metals to form oxides. The nitrogen left behind from the ammonia remains as nitrogen gas (N_2). Thus on any planet no heavier than the Earth, the atmosphere after 4 billion years will consist of nitrogen and carbon dioxide.

By now, 4 billion years later, even the residual nitrogen and carbon dioxide have all escaped from the Moon and Mercury. They have no atmosphere left at all. Mars has lost practically all its nitrogen but does have some residual carbon dioxide, much of it in the form of dry ice around the polar caps. Venus and the Earth have, however, retained all or nearly all of both. The Earth with its liquid water was able to dispose of its carbon dioxide because it went into solution in the water and was converted to solid carbonates, such as limestone, of which the Earth's crust has great quantities. On Venus in the absence of liquid water, the carbon dioxide remained in the atmosphere. At present Venus has about the same amount of nitrogen as the Earth, but she has a crushing mass of carbon dioxide so that the atmospheric pressure at the surface of Venus is over 100 times that on the Earth—nearly a ton per square inch. Under this crushing atmospheric canopy, the temperature at the surface is 800°F, hot enough to melt lead. There may be mountain-forming volcanoes and earthquakes on Venus as there are on the Earth, but without water there has never been any water erosion with resulting sedimentary beds and ore bodies. However, there is probably terrifically powerful wind erosion, with high winds blowing over incredibly hot and totally arid deserts producing sand blasts of an intensity unimagined here. For all the romanticism of which Venus has been the object in human literature, she is as near hell as one can imagine!

II. THE CONDITIONS FOR LIFE ON EARTH

We now turn to the second important point about the hydrogen-containing molecules in the early atmospheres of the planets. As hydrogen atoms were knocked out of them by ultraviolet light, free radicals of carbon, nitrogen, and oxygen were left behind. These are highly active chemically, and they generate in such an atmosphere a great variety of organic compounds basic to life. This process can easily be reproduced in a hydrogen, ammonia, and methane mixture in the laboratory where extended ultraviolet irradiation produces a variety of amino acids, simple sugars, and bases, like adenine, essential to the formation of nucleic acids. On the Earth, and perhaps for a short time on the Moon and Mars as well, these compounds were washed out of the atmosphere by rain from the condensing volcanic steam. As the Earth's oceans grew, they became well stocked in this way with all the basic building blocks of life. The amino acids could join to form proteins, and the sugars and bases when combined with the phosphoric acid dissolved in the water could form nucleic acids such as RNA and DNA. On Mars and the Moon, as the water escaped, these compounds were broken up again and ended up simply as nitrogen and carbon dioxide. On Venus with no liquid water and high temperature, the compounds met the same fate almost as rapidly as they formed.

During the first 1.5 billion years of her history, these organic materials in the growing oceans of the young Earth had somehow become incorporated into simple cellular organisms. This we know from remnants resembling present rod-like bacteria embedded in a black chert 3.2 billion years old in the Fig Tree series of the eastern Transvaal region of Africa. In another billion years a great variety of single-celled filamentous organisms like the modern blue-green algae had developed, as we know from their fossil remains in the Gunflint iron formation on the northern shores of Lake Superior, which is 1.9 billion years old. These organisms were capable of photosynthesis and therefore continually converted carbon dioxide into oxygen in the ocean. For these early organisms the oxygen was highly poisonous, and its presence constituted a major ecological crisis in the history of life. At first their only protection from it was its removal from the oceans by the conversion of soluble ferrous iron to precipitated ferric iron. With this protection there was developed by 1.3 billion years ago a new kind of living cell capable of utilizing the oxidation of sugars as an energy source. The serious oxygen crisis had been successfully passed, and the stage was set for a new development of life of tremendous potential. An impressive record of the oxygen crisis of the period between 2.5 and 1.5 billion years ago is left in the great beds of Lake Superior iron ores and in the Mesabi Range in Minnesota.

For 3.5 billion years of its history, the Earth consisted of oceans and bare, sterile land areas subject to rapid erosion by flowing water. Ultraviolet radiation from the sun was intense over the whole land and sea surface of the Earth. The living organisms in the oceans could never come within several feet of the surface. Those that did were soon destroyed by the ultraviolet radiation. Nothing living existed anywhere on the land. No multicellular organisms or creatures moved through the deep waters throughout that immense period of time. No suspicion of what would later be achieved through the further elaboration of DNA codes, developed by then in the single-celled organisms in the oceans, could have been gained from an examination of the Earth at that time.

The escape of hydrogen from water high in the atmosphere left behind free oxygen, and by 2 billion years ago this was augmented by the free oxygen released in photosynthesis that began to escape from the oceans and join the nitrogen in the Earth's atmosphere. When some 10 percent of the present amount had accumulated around a billion years ago, a layer of ozone was formed high in the atmosphere. This absorbed all of the extreme ultraviolet radiation from the Sun. From then on, living systems could rise to the surface of the oceans and later find habitats on the land. At the same time in response to the dissolved oxygen in the oceans in equilibrium with that in the atmosphere, DNA codes were elaborated for entirely new biological systems for which oxygen was no longer a poison but a benefit. These were the mitochondria that could produce the same essential organic compounds by burning sugar with oxygen as were produced by the ancient and long-standing chloroplasts from carbon dioxide and water using the energy of visible light from the sun. A new and potent energy source was now available for incorporation into living organisms. The stage was set for an astounding new epoch in the Earth's history.

By 650 million years ago, soft-bodied multicellular organisms, jelly-fish, flatworms, and novel animal forms, had developed in the oceans. Their impressions are found in abundance in ancient sandstones in the Ediacora Hills in South Australia. By 600 million years ago, some of these animals had developed the capacity to make calcium carbonate and could cover themselves with hard protective shells. From then on, the history of life on the Earth is recorded in a continuous fossil record. This was the beginning of the geological period known as the Cambrian. The Earth was just 4 billion years old.

The development of living organisms had taken place with almost infinite slowness during those first 4 billion years. In the Cambrian, the rate of development took a quantum jump to a new order of magnitude. Sea creatures developed in great variety and profusion. Plant life began spreading over the land, followed by insects. After 500 million years of such development, the Earth 180 million years ago had acquired a fully developed biosphere with many of the features of today. An Apollo picture of the Earth then would have looked very much the same as one taken now. Closer up, however, the scene then would have been quite different. The dominant creatures were the great reptiles, mighty dinosaurs, immense and fearful flying reptiles, and numerous reptilic sea monsters. There were great coniferous forests and other vegetation clothing the land, but as yet no deciduous hardwoods or flowering plants and shrubs. Also at that time there was no Atlantic Ocean, and Europe and Africa formed a con-tinuous land mass with North and South America.

Just 70 million years ago, the Earth entered a new period of her history called the Tertiary. Most reptiles were extinct, and the age now belonged to the mammals that developed in increasing profusion and variety. Plant life had become much as we know it now. The land was graced with a blanket of verdure, with great hardwood forests and high windswept steppes. There were birds and insects in the air, fish in lakes and rivers, and in the sea. Through forest and prairie, myriads of animals ranged. By the end of the Tertiary just 2 million years ago, these were much the same as we know today: antelopes, zebras, and horses; a va-riety of proboscidians in herds; deer, tigers, wolves, foxes, and badgers. Throughout all of this astonishing efflorescence of the inner energy and dynamism of the phenomenon of life, there was by now in forest and steppe the beauty of flowering plants, shrubs, and trees embracing the whole range of color in every degree of delicacy and brilliance. Only one element was missing from this calm and lovely scene. As yet man had not been produced, and nowhere over the whole earth was there so much as a wisp of smoke rising from a campfire.

III.   THE QUESTION OF LIFE
ON OTHER PLANETS

All science fiction without exception conveys the impression that all planets everywhere throughout the universe are very similar to the Earth. Life has developed on all of them and in each case has finally produced some manlike creature who, although possibly bizarre in appearance, nevertheless thinks, is self-conscious, and can communicate. In addition to science fiction, popular accounts of science in newspapers and magazines instill the same kind of convictions in the readers. A good example is Walter Sullivan's book *We Are Not Alone*.[1] Even some very distinguished and otherwise highly reliable scientists speak this way. Within the scientific community itself, the ideas of the commonness of the Earth and the prevalence of life are widely held. As a result there is as yet in the public at large little appreciation of the extraordinary wonder of the Earth, or of what a rare and precious gem our planet is.

But now against the background of what we know so far of the history of our solar system, let us examine critically the conditions that must be met for anything comparable to the Earth to be achieved anywhere in the universe. First and most essential is liquid water. This, of course, requires a rather narrow temperature range that must persist for at least half the planet's orbit around its star. If the earth were just 10 percent closer to the sun than it is, it would receive 23 percent more solar radiation than it does now. There might then be some liquid water in arctic regions and occasional hot pools elsewhere over the surface that would boil and dry up every summer. There would be some limestone, but the atmosphere would still be like that of Venus with a great amount of carbon dioxide. If the Earth had been 10 percent farther out from the sun, it would receive only 83 percent of the solar energy it does now. In that case most of the water would be in vast ice caps with some melting on the surface of the ice in summer and perhaps some lakes and rivers in the tropics. Again, if the Earth had a highly elliptical orbit around the sun instead of the near circular one it has, the oceans would boil vigorously for two or three months of the year and then freeze solid for six-to-eight months.

If the earth had been much smaller and less massive than it is but otherwise in the same orbit, hydrogen would have escaped much more

[1] New York: McGraw-Hill Book Company, 1964.

rapidly from its gravitational hold. In that event it would not have been able to hold sizable quantities of liquid water for more than 2 or 3 billion years. By now all the water would have escaped along with some of the nitrogen and carbon dioxide. Life could have developed up to the stage of the Gunflint algae perhaps, but then it would have been snuffed out as the last water left. On the other hand, had the Earth been much larger and more massive than it is, it would have retained until now the reducing atmosphere of ammonia and methane plus possibly free hydrogen that seems to have been necessary during its first few billion years for the development of life as we know it. In that case there would be no free oxygen now in the atmosphere and therefore no ozone layer. There would still be no life on the land. How far it would have developed in the deep oceans we have no way of knowing. But the Earth would obviously be a very different place than it is now and with a radically different history.

Those who like to think of the Earth as quite common and unexceptional should contemplate quite deeply the significance of what we know now of the Moon, Mars, and Venus, to say nothing of Jupiter and Saturn. Even in just our own solar system, planets come in a great variety of chemical compositions and physical states. However, their several histories have led after 4.5 billion years to the achievement of nothing like the complexity of organization of matter that we have come to know and take for granted on the Earth.

But it is not only the planet that is important. The central star is also a vital consideration. All main sequence stars like the sun are burning hydrogen into helium in natural "hydrogen bombs" in their cores. When the hydrogen in its core is used up, the star goes into a gravitational collapse that leads to the burning of helium in the core and a tremendous expansion of the outer envelope. The star becomes a red giant. If the star had a system of planets around it, all of these planets would be evaporated and become a part of its outer envelope. This would bring all the planetary histories of whatever character to an abrupt termination. The more massive the star, the more rapid is the burning and the sooner is the red giant stage reached. A star only 50 percent heavier than the sun would reach the red giant stage in 2.3 billion years. If it had a planet the size of the Earth in the right place, life could have developed to the stage of the Gunflint algae before being destroyed. In order to allow a development of at least 4.6 billion years the star must be no more massive than 1.25 times the mass of the sun. The sun itself has several billion years more to go before reaching the red giant stage.

About half the stars are double stars or members of systems of three or more stars. In such multistar systems there are no stable near-circular planetary orbits. The other half of the stars that are single probably have systems of several planets. Moreover there are many more stars less massive than the sun than there are stars that are larger. For example, in our region of space there are three times as many stars with half the mass of the sun as there are stars of the same mass as the sun. These smaller stars are much cooler than the sun, and their radiation is much weaker in ultraviolet. Without ultraviolet both the loss of hydrogen from the original atmosphere would be greatly slowed and the production of organic materials from that atmosphere would be altered. A planet the size of the Earth at the right distance from the star might well develop life, but its evolution over 4 billion years would probably show a very different history. The mechanism of planetary formation around such a star could well favor gaseous planets like Jupiter and Saturn close to the star. Such bodies do not offer an environment favorable to any very elaborate evolution of complex organisms.

There are so many stars now on the main sequence in our galaxy that the probability is large that somewhere another Earth-like planet has held liquid water for billions of years and has enjoyed a history that could have clothed it with verdure and produced another gem of rare beauty like the Earth in the vast reaches of space. But the conditions required for such an outcome, as we have considered them, are such as to suggest that this does not happen very often. Quite possibly there is not another such planet at the stage of development presently reached by the Earth within several hundred light-years of us. If that is the case, then the Earth for all practical purposes is unique. There is no other creative achievement of such a high organization of matter within any conceivable reach of us.

IV. THE ADVENT OF MAN

The preceding account of the history of the Earth went through the Tertiary to the beginning of the present geological epoch, the Pleistocene, just 2 million years ago. This was purposely done in order to bring out the major character of the turning point in this long history that the appearance of man on the planet represents. Only three or four other turning points of comparable magnitude can be identified. One was certainly the point over 3 billion years ago at which nucleic acid and protein first became organized in living cells. The second was the achievement of photosynthesis around 2.5 billion years ago with its attendant oxygen crisis. The third was the transformation 600 million years ago from the pre-Cambrian to the Cambrian when multicellular organisms appeared and the Earth began to acquire a biosphere. A fourth could have been the capture of the Moon by the Earth sometime between these two turning points, followed by its subsequent close approach to the Earth with immense, scouring tidal waves. The fifth is the very recent appearance of man as a result of which the Earth has acquired what Teilhard de Chardin aptly calls the "noosphere"—i.e., a pervasive clothing of the earth in a blanket of mind and spirit. The planetary impact and crisis proportions of this transformation of the biosphere into the noosphere are just beginning to be felt in this century.

Early in the Pleistocene one stem of the evolving and diversifying branch of primates took a fateful step. As in so many other points in the history of life, a door opened briefly and this primate stepped through it; had he passed by instead to go through some other door, the opportunity for man could well have been passed up forever. The result was the first of the species *Homo*. He left the trees and began to learn to walk on two feet. He originated in south central Africa and is called *Homo habilis*. After a long period of continuous development and diversification, a quite new version called *Homo erectus* appeared on the scene 300,000 years ago, after which all forms of *Homo habilis* became extinct. In time *Homo erectus* showed the very human trait of wanderlust, and he migrated to the Middle East, Europe, England, China, and Southeast Asia. In Europe he is Heidelberg man, in China Sinanthropus, and in Java Pithecanthropus. By 100,000 years ago a still more human version, *Homo neanderthalensis*, emerged. He is the first creature in the whole history of life on earth to have buried his dead. From this fact alone we know we are dealing with a self-conscious being who anticipates in anxiety or hope. Yet if we could see a Neanderthal man today with his massive jaw and absence of forehead, we would not consider him human at all.

Then some 40,000 years ago one of the diversifying lines of development in Neanderthal man made another leap, and our species *Homo sapiens* first appeared on the scene; with his arrival *Homo neanderthalensis* became extinct. This new species not only buried his dead but was an artist as well, and we still marvel at the remarkable dynamic paintings of mammoth and reindeer he left in the caves of southern France. But for the next 30,000 years he remained a hunter and gatherer of food like other animals and did not appreciably alter the balance of nature into which he was born. Then some 10,000 years ago a drastic change began to materialize in his way of life. Settled villages were formed based on the first agriculture and domestication of animals. In another 5,000 years, another major step was taken in the emergence of the first civilizations in Egypt and Mesopotamia, which led to cities, nations, and empires, with a division of labor from slave to king, and attendant professions. Then, just 200 years ago the industrial revolution ushered in a new era of mechanical power and invention leading in the last 50 years to an efflorescence in science and technology, consumption and pollution, and above all population explosion. By now there is widespread recognition of the fact that the noosphere is interacting in a major and decisive way with the biosphere and that this interaction is bound to reach a crisis level before the end of this century.

Several aspects of this crisis call for consideration against the background of the total history of the Earth as it has been outlined here. Perhaps the first of these that stands out is the extraordinary acceleration that the phenomenon of life has manifested in its history. Some sense of this acceleration is made evident by the accompanying table.

HISTORY OF LIFE ON EARTH

Measured in Stages in the Years before 2000 AD

	Historical Epoch
4,600,000,000	
	Chemical evolution of protein and nucleic acid.
3,200,000,000	
	Development of living cells in reducing conditions, dependent on fermentation and feeding on each other.
2,500,000,000	
	Blue-green algae develop photosynthesis and nitrogen fixation. Crisis of oxygen.
1,500,000,000	
	Development of respiratory cells using oxygen for energy. Oxygen in atmosphere. Ozone layer shields ultraviolet. Life comes to surface of sea.
650,000,000	
	Multicellular organisms and macroscopic animals develop in seas. Plants and then animal life cover the land. Coal, oil, and natural gas produced.
230,000,000	
	Dinosaurs and other reptiles. Hardwoods and shrubs.
70,000,000	
	Mammals, grasses, flowers, fruits, and vegetables. Production of the modern world other than man.
2,000,000	
	Appearance of man from most primitive through Neanderthal man.
40,000	
	Homo sapiens as hunter and gatherer.
10,000	
	Rural farm villages.

5,000	
	Cities, nations, empires. Written language and literature.
200 (1800 AD)	
	Industrial revolution, mechanical power, and machinery.
80 (1920 AD)	
	Age of affluence, science, and technology.
30 (1970 AD)	
	Population explosion and ecological crisis in the biosphere. Beginning of Postcivilization.
0 (2000 AD)	

What stands out in this table is the extraordinary compression in the time scale that has marked each new stage in the history of life. Measured first in billion-year periods, it moves to 100 million-, to 10 million-, to million-year spans. Thereafter for man it goes from 100,000- to 10,000-year spans, and then from millenia, to centuries, to mere decades. The acceleration of life has become breathtaking if not intolerable. We do indeed live in a time of change more rapid by orders of magnitude than any that the phenomenon of life on this planet has ever experienced before.

Another feature that stands out is the immense potentiality of matter as organized on the Earth to rise to ever and ever more complex modes of organization culminating in the phosphorescence of thought and spirit that now clothes the Earth in her noosphere. In a companion contribution to this volume, Daniel Day Williams emphasizes the concept of possibility as a fundamental new understanding of both man and nature. What stands out here is the extreme rarity of conditions throughout the universe in which this inherent almost unlimited potentiality of matter can be realized. One need only think of the Moon, Mars, and Mercury to find matter severely limited in possibility. Jupiter and Saturn may consist almost entirely of hydrogen and helium and, although for them such possibilities, unknown to us, as solid helium and metallic hydrogen are actualized, additional possibilities for new developments of matter are almost nonexistent. Matter in stars can occasionally be assembled into the rare and unusual forms of atoms heavier than iron all the way to uranium and californium when the star becomes a supernova. But for the most part it is severely limited in the variety of possibilities open to it regardless of the length of time available.

Because of this, philosophies based on process and becoming, on the openness of history to new possibilities and potentialities, are probably peculiar to man and to his Earth and to the extremely rare places elsewhere in the universe where similar stringent conditions are satisfied. For the universe as a whole, and practically the whole of matter in it, they have very little relevance or significance.

V. THE FUTURE OF MAN

Finally we must consider in the light of what we know now, the significance for the future of life on Earth of the creation of *Homo sapiens* in the recent evolution of primates. Was this destiny-laden step in the long history of life a move upward or a catastrophe? The anthropologist Loren Eiseley in his book *The Firmament of Time*[2] considers that the evolutionary forces that have driven the elaboration of DNA codes throughout the history of life made a fatal blunder when they produced man. Up to then, life had been progressing to ever higher and higher levels until at the end of the Tertiary the Earth had been clothed in a mantle of wondrous beauty. The introduction of man into this calm and balanced scene is proving to be a lethal factor for it. In an especially powerful passage, Eiseley says:

> It is with the coming of man that a vast hole seems to open in nature, a vast black whirlpool spinning faster and faster, consuming flesh, stones, soil, minerals, sucking down the lightning, wrenching power from the atom, until the ancient sounds of nature are drowned in the cacophony of something which is no longer nature, something instead which is loose and knocking at the world's heart, something demonic and no longer planned—escaped, it may be—spewed out of nature, contending in a final giant's game against its master.

Indeed when one considers the present state of the Earth, the planet is profoundly threatened by man in many ways. Reserves of fossil fuel laid down over a span of 100 million years, especially of petroleum and natural gas, are being rapidly exhausted. Spills pollute the surface of the ocean, and in burning these fuels the Earth's atmosphere is being polluted and its carbon dioxide is steadily rising. The lakes and rivers that so recently graced the Earth are being made unfit for either man or fish. The wilderness is shrinking and being converted into either vast urban sprawls or junk heaps. Many strange and wonderful species of living things have already become extinct since man appeared, and many hundreds more are rapidly approaching extinction. All other living things are finding life more and more difficult in the face of man. Perhaps it is true that any planet anywhere in the universe that acquires a noosphere is courting catastrophe.

[2]New York: Atheneum Publishers, 1962.

Two well-known Biblical passages have a new significance in the light of our current situation. The first is the remarkably perceptive summary of man's destiny at the end of the first chapter of Genesis: "So, God created man in his own image, and blessed them and said to them, 'Be fruitful and multiply and fill the earth and subdue it; and have dominion over the fish of the sea, and over the birds of the air, and over the cattle, and over the whole earth'" (1:26–28). In this last half of the twentieth century we are seeing this destiny fulfilled before our eyes to a degree that no previous generation could have believed possible. By the end of the century the human population will have reached the limit that the Earth is capable of supporting, and man will indeed have "filled the earth." The full flowering of science and technology in this century is making it literally possible for man for the first time in his history to really "subdue the earth" and exercise effective dominion over all other creatures. There are profound theological implications in this passage that our present perspective on man and on his relation to the Earth are just now beginning to make evident.

The other relevant passage is from Deuteronomy and deals with the implications of man's freedom in his exercise of dominion: "Behold I set before you this day life and death, blessing and curse; therefore choose life" (30:19). Up to now, as Loren Eiseley has so powerfully shown, man has used his dominion to curse the Earth and her other creatures, and the outcome of the curse can only be death for both the creatures and himself. But it does not have to be this way. Man can exercise his dominion in a way that blesses the Earth and assists her to reach levels of development that she could never have achieved without him. I have personally experienced a striking example of this potentiality through the opportunity to observe at firsthand the transformation wrought by the Tennessee Valley Authority since the early 1930s in the East Tennessee region in which I have lived during this period. This kind of exercise of dominion in love is what René Dubos has so aptly called an active "wooing" of the Earth. It can indeed be a great blessing to both man and nature.

The problem that confronts us most urgently is whether mankind throughout the world can change sufficiently radically in time to convert the present curse into a blessing. My own view is that he will not do so until he has suffered greatly and much that he now relies upon has been destroyed. As the Earth in a short few decades becomes twice as crowded with human beings as it is now, and as human societies are confronted with dwindling resources in the midst of mounting accumulations of wastes and a steadily deteriorating environment, we can only foresee social paroxysms of an intensity greater than any we have so far known. The problems are so varied and so vast and the means for their solution so far beyond the resources of the scientific and technological know-how on which we have relied that there simply is not time to avoid the impending castrophe. We stand, therefore, on the threshold of a time of judgment more severe, undoubtedly, than any that mankind has ever faced before in history.

There is, however, hope in such a situation. In human history as well as in the history of life as a whole, times of judgment and of great dying have been preludes to great new creative achievements. One senses that the rest of this century will see the destruction of civilization as we have known it for the past 5,000 years, with its warring nation-states and its exploitation of human and natural resources. Civilization will then be seen in retrospect as simply a 5,000-year stage in the development of man comparable to the 5,000-year stage of the settled village agricultural societies that preceded it. What will take its place we do not presently have the experience to perceive. Postcivilization will be a new creation, just as civilization was at its birth. One vision of what it might be like is developed in the contribution to this book by Harold Schilling. Whatever it is to be, however, it is probably true that it cannot even begin to come into being until what we have now is destroyed. That is the meaning of times of judgment in history. They are necessary to the achievement of the creative aims of the transcendent purpose that has so evidently been at work throughout the whole incredibly long history of life on this planet.

It is awesome to contemplate the immense creative investment that has gone into bringing the Earth to her present stage of beauty and fulfillment. The slow but ever-accelerating elaboration of information coded on DNA over an unimaginably vast reach of time has by now produced, suspended in the alien reaches of space, a magic garden and placed within it that strangest achievement of any of the manifold DNA codes—man. This was possible because of a most delicate balance of gravity, heat, and light realized on the Earth, a balance achieved only very rarely, if at all, on other planets. This uniqueness and the wonder of the creative achievement that it has made possible mean that the Earth is a rare gem of fantastic beauty, and that its desecration or destruction by any being is an act of awful sacrilege against which the heart of all meaning and purpose in the entire universe must cry out in anguish.

If, as I believe to be the case, the human species stands on the threshold of the next great step in its evolution, then this view of the Earth may well prove to be a decisive element in the possibility of that step. A full appreciation of not only the beauty but of the holiness of the Earth and of the immense creative investment that has gone into producing it, including as an integral component man himself, is essential to man's continued occupation of this planet. With such an appreciation man will know how to love the Earth as she is indeed worthy of love, to woo

her into ever greater and more wonderful creative achievements, to celebrate the wonder of the achievement already realized, and to have a holy
fear of desecrating her. To do this it is first necessary for man widely and
generally to recover his lost sense of transcendent reality. The process of
this recovery is well underway and will be much accelerated during the
time of judgment that is now upon us, with its destruction of secular hopes
and confidences and its acute raising of the issues of meaning and purpose.
As men regain this essentially theological perspective on nature and on
their proper place within it, they will be enabled to respond more and
more fully to the creative energies now at work in the world, and to play
their part in bringing into being the new creation that is now in prepara-
tion. For those meek enough to be guided in judgment, the prospect of
what is coming on the world in the remainder of this century does not
lead to despair. Rather their hope is deeply grounded in and sustained by
the knowledge that the creative energy that has been able to accomplish
such amazing results through a 4.5 billion-year history is not presently
exhausted. In concert with man, that same energy is even now at work
preparing the next great step in this long process.

The future is of course unpredictable in principle. The history of the
remainder of the century must have the same character as all past history.
It will have many surprises and unpredictable turning points that will
decisively influence the turn of events thereafter. But there are at the
same time a few "givens" that are so fundamental that we can be confident they will be primary shapers of that history. The first and most
important is the population explosion that guarantees regardless of what
we do now that there will be nearly twice as many of us at the end of
the century as there are now. The effect of this immense crowding in the
Middle East, India, Pakistan, China, Africa, and Central and South America is clearly ominous.

Another is the fact that in the developed countries ever since the
industrial revolution gross national products; energy production; water
requirements; the production of solid, liquid, and gaseous wastes; and
the consumption of irreplaceable resources of fossil fuels and metals have
all been increasing exponentially. A simple projection of these exponential curves to the end of the century leads to predictable impossibilities.
This is particularly true of electric power, fresh water requirements, volumes of wastes to be disposed of, and consumption of petroleum, natural
gas, mercury, copper, molybdenum, and some other metals. Exponential
growth curves can never in nature be continued indefinitely. At some
point each such curve must decrease its rate of increase and begin leveling
off or, in the case of limited resources, decrease. For different components
this will happen at different times.

In the seventies the pressing problems all over the world will be waste disposal and pollution control. In the eighties they will be fresh water and food. In the nineties they will be the approaching exhaustion of petroleum, natural gas, helium, and several key metals. Gross national products will be leveling off all over the world, and consumption by a greatly expanded population will be sharply decreased by then. It will begin to be realized that the industrial revolution was only a brief period in human history; a two-hundred-year joy ride that was wonderful while it lasted.

During this whole period of painful readjustment to the realities of man's intricate involvement in the whole order of nature and her ecological balance, there are bound to be social strains of ever-growing intensity. These will certainly be severe in the seventies in the Middle East and Southeast Asia. They seem unavoidable by the eighties in Africa and Central and South America and perhaps also in India, Pakistan, and China with their immense and hungry populations. There is no telling about North America, Europe, Russia, and Japan throughout this same period. At this point one's vision fails.

Such an analysis of our present predicament defines the balance of this century as a time of severe judgment for all mankind. The adjustment to it will be painful and agonizing, but there is no escape from it. It will see the end of the golden age of science, of galloping technology in the service of unbridled consumption and affluence, and of many of our most cherished institutions. The affluent society will be no more. Many important materials will have been nearly exhausted and will be very expensive. But man will still have an abundance of energy at his command and a highly sophisticated technology with which to build a new world. That new world will have to be based on a stable or even decreasing population and a stable, nonincreasing gross national product. It will minimize individual consumption and redirect production toward general communal needs in transportation, housing, food production, environmental quality, and recreation. It can be a much more humane world, expressive of the essential unity of mankind and organized along very different lines than those that have characterized the civilizations of the past 5,000 years. It is this that leads me to believe that we presently stand on the threshold of the decline of civilization as the typical mode of organization of mankind and the emergence of an entirely new type—a postcivilization. The only way the new world of postcivilization has a chance to be born is for the existing structures, institutions, and power networks of civilization to be cleared away. That is the meaning of the time of judgment that faces us in the remainder of this century. Such periods have happened before in the history of man, and in retrospect we know that they have not been without hope and promise.

WILLIAM G. POLLARD is Executive Director, Oak Ridge Associated Universities, Oak Ridge, Tennessee, having gone there in 1947 as the first director. He previously taught physics at the University of Tennessee and is an ordained priest in the Episcopal Church. He is coauthor of The Hebrew Iliad *and author of* Chance and Providence, Physicist and Christian, Atomic Energy and Southern Science, Man on a Spaceship, *and* Science and Faith: Twin Mysteries.

HAROLD K. SCHILLING

7

The Whole Earth Is the Lord's

toward a holistic ethic

Many thoughtful people have come to feel that the pollution and destruction of man's environment are religious and ethical problems that derive basically from irreverent and immoral attitudes toward nature, rather than from technological inadequacy alone. They feel that the solution is not beyond the capabilities of technology—provided it allows itself to be guided by more sensitive religious views and ethical motivations with respect to nature than now prevail generally in our culture. I share this view.

Too long has man acted as though the earth belonged to him to do with as he pleased, without regard for the rights of nature and of its inhabitants; and too often has he, at least in the West, defended this attitude by appealing to the biblical doctrine of man's dominion over the earth—as though God had foreordained him to be its owner and master in an autocratic sense. For the religious community this poses the difficult question of how this situation can be rectified. I suggest, however, that what it may have to say will not be convincing until it has developed a much more adequate religious understanding of nature than it now possesses. Fortunately, there is now available much scientific knowledge about the fundamental character of reality that promises to be of the utmost value for the development of such an understanding. It is in the light of these newer insights that I shall present my thesis. What these

100

insights help us to sense is that, religiously speaking, not only are all things in the world the Lord's, but it is the world in its wholeness that is His. It is my suggestion that the recognition of this can provide the rationale for a satisfactory ethic of man's relationship to nature.

I. THE HOLISTIC
VIEW OF NATURE

1. MAN NOT SEPARATE FROM NATURE

The new knowledge constitutes what is increasingly being called "the new scientific world view." It is a grand vision that is transforming radically men's thinking, behavior, faiths, and hopes, as well as their very consciousness and conscience. Nowhere is this more evident than in the contemporary awareness of the holistic character of the world. All of its components—its fundamental entities, its soil and mineral deposits, its atmosphere and waters, its plants, animals, and human beings—all these together are seen to constitute an integrated ecosystem (ecological system) by virtue of their dynamic interrelations, interactions, and mutually supportive functions. Because of this vision the traditional forms of atomism, reductionism, and the like have become utterly untenable, and the ideas of relationship, interdependence, and wholeness have been elevated to the status of primary categories in contemporary thought.

Let us now consider some of the more important features of this new vision, beginning with its concept of men, where the contrast between the old and new views is especially striking. First, man has discovered that he is in no sense separate from nature, as he formerly supposed, but is integrally a part of it. Everything he is and does, including his culture —with its arts, sciences, and religions, as well as his psychological and social existence—is deeply embedded in the system we call nature and is subject to its laws. More than that, man realizes that he is so completely a part of his immediate environment that his very personhood derives in large measure from its effects upon him.

Take, for instance, his intellect or mind, i.e., his capacity to think and reason. We now know that this does not come to him simply because he is born with a human genetic endowment and is thus destined inevitably to have a mind; rather it comes into being gradually through his interaction with his environment. At birth a normal baby has a brain, a nervous system, and the usual senses for perception; but, so far as we know, it has no mind. For, unlike the brain or heart, the mind is not an organ of the body; it is a function or process that comes into being and develops, along with the whole personality, as the body receives and reacts to stimuli, signals, and information from its environment. If soon after birth the baby were isolated, say in a dark and soundless cell, so that no stimuli could reach it from the outside, it would become no more than a mass of protoplasm, perhaps with a human form if it were properly fed, but certainly not with a mind. It would become what is often called "only a vegetable." Geertz, anthropologist at the University of Chicago, puts it rather incisively this way:

> There is no such thing as a human nature independent of culture. Men without culture would not be the clever savages of Golding's *Lord of the Flies*, thrown back upon the cruel wisdom of their animal instincts; nor would they be the nature's noblemen of Enlightenment primitivism, or even, as classical anthropological theory would imply, intrinsically talented apes who had somehow failed to find themselves. They would be unworkable monstrosities with very few useful instincts, fewer recognizable sentiments, and no intellect; mental basket cases.[1]

Man has probably always known that he depends utterly upon his environment for the so-called absolute necessities of his physical existence, such as air, water, and food. Recently, however, he has discovered that he is directly dependent upon it also for his mentality. For, as Platt of the University of Michigan explains, there is also the absolute necessity

> throughout our waking life for a continuous novelty and variety of external stimulation of our eyes, ears, sense organs and all our nervous network. . . . Our brains organize, and exist to organize, a great variety of incoming sensory messages every waking second, and can become not only emotionally upset but seriously deranged if these messages cease or even if they cease to be new. New experience is not merely a childish want; it is something we cannot do without.[2]

Our minds are not only culture-dependent, but nature-dependent as well. For without the realities of nature, such as light and sound, smell, heat, and pressure, there could be no transmission of signals; and without objects of nature, such as the warbling birds, blossoming cherry trees, sighing wind, and speaking humans, there would be no sources of signals —and thus no intellects. No nature, then no human quality of existence! Without nature there would be no human souls in the biblical sense of the

---

[1]Clifford Geertz, "The Impact of the Concept of Culture," in John R. Platt, ed., *New Views of the Nature of Man* (Chicago: University of Chicago Press, 1965), pp. 112ff.
[2]John R. Platt, *The Excitement of Science* (Boston: Houghton Mifflin Company, 1962), Chap. 5, pp. 64ff.

human psychosomatic wholes that we call, in modern parlance, persons. As nature changes in its future evolution, so will mankind; and it remains to be seen what the term "man" will mean in the tomorrows. In any case, his humanhood has existence and character not separately or of itself but only relationally.

2. THE RELATIONAL CHARACTER OF PHYSICAL REALITY

Second, what has been said about the relational nature of man applies to all reality known to science, namely, that its entities exist and are definable primarily by virtue of interrelationships with other entities, rather than by virtue of any supposed substance-essences of their own. Their fundamental properties are not so much inherent as derivative; and this is the case even where, in terms of older views, it was expected least, namely, in matter. Wood, for instance, is said to be a complex of fundamental substances, among which is the chemical element carbon. This is familiar to us in the form of charcoal, a chunk of which consists of billions of carbon atoms. If in the nineteenth century one had asked what a carbon atom is, the reply would have been that it is simply a bit of a primordial substance called carbon; and this would have seemed self-evident and quite sufficient as an answer.

At present it would not seem so, for now atoms are known to consist of subatomic entities, such as electrons, protons, neutrons. If in turn, we asked what these are made of, we would get the seemingly frustrating answer that this is not a meaningful question when applied to the interior of atoms. For as scientists have probed deeper and deeper into matter— say a bit of charcoal—they have found virtually nothing there that reminds them of unchanging "substance." Rather they have found atoms to be dynamic, undulating structures, which often remind one more of waves than of pellets, and within which occur many sorts of strange events. Thus it has become much more meaningful—and far less frustrating—to think of an electron, say, in terms of dynamic interrelations and events or of behavior patterns rather than in terms of substance. The electron is an entity that behaves in a certain way in the presence of other entities; a neutron behaves in a different way, and a proton in still another way. These specifiable behaviors result from correspondingly specifiable dynamic interrelationships (forces and fields) among entities, which make themselves manifest through various kinds of events caused by them. It is in this sense that the properties of a so-called building block of matter are derivative. In our time, then, to ask what an entity *is* fundamentally, is to ask not what it is made of but how it interacts with others. This is the meaning of the assertion that matter and all other physical reality are basically relational and eventful.

3. THE DRIVE TOWARD AGGREGATION
AND WHOLENESS

A third feature of physical reality is that its fundamental units display a drive toward the formation of ever larger and more complex structures, which have properties not possessed by the constituting individuals, and which are therefore the properties of wholes only, and not of parts. To illustrate, carbon atoms may join others to produce carbon molecules, which tend to aggregate in large numbers to produce carbon in bulk, e.g., charcoal or graphite or diamonds. Or they may join with oxygen atoms to produce carbon dioxide molecules, which may then congregate to produce carbon dioxide in bulk, as a gas, liquid, or solid (depending upon the temperature). In both cases there emerge from the aggregation or union new realities, namely, the qualities of matter in bulk that do not characterize the individual carbon atoms. Among these are opaque blackness (in the case of charcoal), transparency and lustre (diamond), and white translucency (carbon dioxide snow). A different class of emergents is represented by solidity and liquidity, with subsidiary properties like hardness, softness, elasticity, tensile strength, viscosity. The point to be stressed is that none of these properties of matter exists except where many molecules congregate. There is no such thing as a black or white molecule— or atom. Color and temperature and other such qualities of matter belong to larger wholes only.

In an analogous manner, individual human beings display a drive toward aggregation in social communities, which as wholes also have characteristics different from those of their constituents. Thus a man cannot be a politician by himself, nor an educator. Politics, education, commerce, and the like are phenomena and qualities of the social rather than the solitary life; and so are school spirit, patriotism, and mob rule, to cite radically different examples. These come into being only when many individual persons congregate or unite in closely knit groups or communities.

It is a most remarkable fact that virtually everything we prize most is of this type. Without this holistic thrust toward systemic structure and community, and the interrelationships and emergents that derive from them, life would be terribly empty. There would be no parenthood, brotherhood, friendship, citizenship; no language and literature, no science and philosophy, no jurisprudence and economics; no knowledge, or wisdom, or loyalty and love. All of these qualities are strictly social in kind, and they are not available or possible to the isolated individual who is not "in community." Thus wholeness and the drive toward systemic unity reveal themselves to be extremely important aspects of the world and fundamental elements of reality. Nature is thus seen to be essentially social in character.

4. MIND AND SPIRIT IN NATURE

One of the most significant features of the contemporary understanding of the world is that man is not the only being in nature with mind and spirit. Certainly animals display both characteristics and often to an amazing degree. In considering this, let us clarify the meaning of these terms by reference first to the case of *Homo sapiens*. Man's *mind*, I take it, is his intellect, that process or function of his psychosomatic wholeness by which he reasons and solves the problems that confront him in life. The term *spirit*, on the other hand, refers to the "power of life," or "the power of animation"—to use Tillich's potent phrases[3]—or to the passionate will to live, the zest and exuberance of life. A man has spirit when he is spirited. The term spirit also refers to man's trans-intellectual capacity for sensitivity, compassion, and insight *in depth*, and to that creativity to which we refer when we speak of works of art as "the creations of the human spirit"—not just as the creations of the human mind. To speak of Gandhi, Einstein, and Schweitzer as simply *great minds* would somehow seem quite inadequate, even though they were giant intellects. They were much more, namely, *great spirits*—truly sensitive, understanding, concerned, and compassionate. According to these usages, both mind and spirit are natural dimensions of life itself, not separate essences or ethereal substances added to it. This understanding rejects utterly the Cartesian dualisms of matter and mind, or matter and spirit; and makes way for the idea that mind and spirit, like life itself, are the outcomes of normal growth in the lifetime of an individual and of the long-range evolutionary development of the world.

In what sense, then, may animals be said to possess mind and spirit? Animals solve problems with varying degrees of ingenuity, and thus they have minds. They have spirit in that they may be intensely vital, passionately spirited, or truly compassionate, and they may show concerned understanding. They have calls for help to which they respond and surrender signals that they respect. It was once thought that evolutionary advances in nature occurred largely in blood and gore, by saber tooth and claw, i.e., by destructive competition; and we are all aware that there is

[3]Paul Tillich, *Systematic Theology III* (Chicago: University of Chicago Press, 1963), pp. 21ff.

very much of this even now. Nevertheless, today's biologists find much evidence that the "morality of nature" is characterized mainly by symbiotic cooperation and mutual aid. Out of this new understanding has come a keen sense of man's spiritual kinship with the animals and an intensified awareness of the common evolutionary heritage he shares with them.

To illustrate this more concretely, I present the following story about three dolphins, a story that was first told as evidence of the high order of their intelligence or mind. To me, however, it also indicates a remarkable spirit, which manifests itself in the will of the ailing dolphin to fight off death, and in the keen concern and intelligent response of its fellows that go to its rescue and stay by it until they win out.

> The episode involved a dolphin that, during an experiment, apparently became so chilled that it was unable to swim. Placed back in the main tank with two other dolphins, it sank to the bottom, where it was bound to suffocate unless it could reach the surface to breathe. However, it gave the distress call and the other two immediately lifted its head until the blowhole was out of water, so that it could take a deep breath. It then sank and a great deal of whistling and twittering took place among the three animals. The two active ones than began swimming past the other so that their dorsal fins swept over its ano-genital region in a manner that caused a reflex contraction of the fluke muscles, much as one can make a dog scratch itself by rubbing the right spot on its flank. The resultant action of the flukes lifted the animal to the surface and the procedure was repeated for several hours until the ailing dolphin had recovered.[4]

It would be difficult indeed for any sensitive person to ponder this moving story without coming to feel deeply that here the human spirit meets another spirit, the animal spirit, and that it is a genuine spirit, and therefore not wholly different in kind.

The point of this discussion, however, is not only that animals possess spirit, but that mind and spirit, as well as life, are now known to be natural aspects of our environmental ecosystem—rather than essentially extra- or supra-natural and presumably immortal entities injected into physical bodies at birth or conception by special acts of God. Thus, mind and spirit are emergents from wholes, just as are color, heat, hardness, electrical conductivity, and other such qualities as we have been considering. Mind and spirit understood as emergents from living organisms represent the most advanced developments of evolution—thus far—and the most meaningful content of nature. And the highest of these is spirit, for it is here that we encounter the animation and passions of life, artistic creative-

---

[4] Walter Sullivan, *We Are Not Alone*, rev. ed. (New York: The New American Library, Inc., Signet Books, 1966), p. 245.

ness, sympathy and empathy, the power of love, compassion, and sacrifice —and much else without which human life and the cosmos as a whole would be largely meaningless. And it is here that men have discerned the most convincing intimations of ultimate meaning and value and reality. Here too we encounter that quality of man through which he becomes aware of the sacrality of nature. It is through the spirit that man is enabled to perceive that an ethical imperative must follow from the sense of what is sacred and should not be tampered with irresponsibly.

II. AN ETHIC OF MAN'S ACTION IN NATURE

1. DESPOLIATION, DESECRATION, BLASPHEMY

Now let us return to the dolphins, and suppose that someone came along with the urge to fish for one of these magnificent creatures, to exhibit it eventually in his trophy room. What might this do to the spirits of the other two? Or suppose some toxic wastes from a paper mill were dumped into the dolphins' habitation, and we had to watch the choking animals search desperately for clean water. How would a truly human spirit react to such a deed? And how would the universe, and God?

There are those who would say that such talk is sheer sentimentality; witness the following pronouncement by one scientist whom Eiseley quotes:

Balance of nature? An outmoded biological concept. There is no room for sentiment in modern science. We shall learn to get along without the birds if necessary. After all, the dinosaurs disappeared. Man merely makes the process go faster. Everything changes in time.

Many others, however, would deny this vehemently, and reply with Eiseley:

And so it does. But let us be as realistic as the gentleman would wish. It may be we who go. I am just primitive enough to hope that somehow, somewhere, a cardinal may still be whistling on a green bush when the last man goes blind before his man-made sun. If it should turn out that we have mishandled our lives as several civilizations before us have done, it seems a pity that we should involve the violet and the tree frog in our departure. To perpetrate this final act of malice seems somehow disproportionate beyond endurance. It is like tampering with the secret purposes

of the universe itself and involving not just man but life in the final holocaust—an act of petulant, deliberate blasphemy.[5]

Surely, it must be evident that these words, far from representing shallow
sentimentality, express deep religious and ethical sensitivity, as well as
profound insight. It is a sensing that we are indeed talking about blasphemy—an irresponsible, diabolic "tampering" with "the secret purposes"
and fundamental relational and holistic realities of the cosmos, and an
arrogant violating of what is sacred and infinitely precious to the God of
the universe. This is what pollution is, as is the littering of the earth and
outer space, the wasting of natural resources, the wanton destruction of
plant and animal life, the irresponsible upsetting of ecological equilibria,
the crushing of human and nonhuman spirit. All of this is blasphemy at
its worst!

To speak of blasphemy in this situation is to be religiously sensitive
in two ways: first, to the sanctity of natural relationships, and second, to
the evil and sacrilegious side of man. The former is not, of course, unrelated to Schweitzer's deep reverence for life, where nature is discerned
to be God's creation and the object of his affection. And this perspective is
not alien to the feeling and insight of St. Francis that the birds, the
flowers, the wolves, and the sun were his brothers under God. Not a few
men, both inside and outside of the professional science community, have
come to see nature in this light and to feel therefore an urgent need for
an ethic of man's responsibility to nature—one that derives from men's
sense of the sacrality of nature.

As to the second point, there has been developing, for basically the
same reasons, keen awareness of that dark and unfortunate side of man's
character that reveals itself in his inhumane treatment of nature and its
inhabitants. Loren Eiseley has called this to our attention with prophetic
insight and fervor, saying that man has shown himself to be "the lethal
factor" in nature, one that has callously and arrogantly damaged and
disfigured much of the landscape, making it "unnatural," destroying its
ecological balance, and even threatening to incinerate it utterly. Eiseley
speaks of the aggregate result of these outrages as a "vast black whirlpool"
that is turning faster and faster, threatening to drag downward into
oblivion both man and his world.[6] Eiseley is not alone in this judgment.
This painful awareness of man's lethal and sacrilegious character provides
the second urgent reason why we must develop the new kind of ethic
being called for here.

[5]Loren Eiseley, "Man, the Lethal Factor," *American Scientist* (March 1963),
pp. 78ff.

[6]Loren Eiseley, *The Firmament of Time* (New York: Atheneum Publishers,
1966), p. 123–24.

2. THE NEED FOR A HOLISTIC
ETHICAL STANCE

What kind of an ethic should it be? Thinking only about its possible general features, my first suggestion is that it should be holistic in conception and thrust, thus recognizing that wholeness and the system of interrelationships are of ultimate significance for the cosmic scheme of things. This ethic should declare itself for the conservation and enhancement of wholeness where it exists and to the redemption or healing of it where it has been broken. Those decisions and actions that bring about maximization of such interrelation and interdependence as make for wholeness should therefore be designated as morally responsible and right, and those that operate to break or destroy it should be regarded as wrong.

Such an ethic would accept the inevitability of tension between individual and group, between what is best for the individual and what is best for the common good, and would seek a balance between the two by emphasizing the needs, not of the individual in and of himself, but of the *individual in community*. This would be recognizing the supremacy of relatedness, interdependence, and wholeness, rather than of independence, self-sufficiency, and isolation; and of communality, rather than of rugged individualism. Also it would be taking cognizance of the great fact of natural existence that the individual—human and nonhuman— derives existence, character, and meaning from the relationships that make up the community.

Although some implications of these principles are obvious, others are not, and they need special emphasis. One is that our sense of the iniquity of environmental pollution must not stem only from our fear of its consequences for ourselves. The animals too must breathe, and so must the plants; hence they too have rights here. It is the *whole earth* that is being damaged. Even if man could somehow avoid serious damage to himself, a holistic ethic would demand his acting vigorously to protect his fellow creatures if they were endangered—as indeed they are.

The biblical ethic has had an essentially twofold focus, calling for love of God and love of neighbor. It should now become threefold, demanding also love of nature. This would not violate biblical insight. Jesus said that his Father loves the lilies of the field, and clothes them with great splendor. Nor is God unaware of the anguish of the universe, "groaning in all its parts." And it is the whole planet to which the transformative, redemptive action of God is directed. Christians should not forget that God "sent his only begotten Son" because he "loved *the world*"—not only us, mankind. Surely our love and ethic should not be concerned any less with *the world*—as a whole!

3. PROXIMATE PRINCIPLES, SITUATIONAL "COMMANDMENTS"

It seems always to have been necessary to translate general ultimate principles into more specific proximate ones, to serve as practical guidelines for decision making in typical situations; hence the codes of the great law givers of history. Without such concrete interpretation, abstract ideals mean little to most people. Thus, although men may agree that one should love one's neighbor, they may disagree radically on what this entails in various contexts. Among the Hebrews such interpretational principles appeared as the Ten Commandments, which became definitive throughout the West. Here the twofold focus is apparent, the first four edicts referring to man's relations with God, and the last six to those with his fellow men. Together they covered essentially all of the important moral problems that Western man has had for over two millennia. Today, however, there are large areas of life to which they do not speak directly, for instance, man's behavior toward his nonhuman environment. Hence we urgently need to develop new commandments to indicate what the ethical demand to love nature may mean situationally.

It will not do, however, to formulate such proximate principles as unqualified prohibitions (you-shall-nots), as though they were to be taken as inflexible absolutes. Contemporary man has become very much aware of the ambiguity found in nature, and this must be reflected in a certain amount of elasticity in the language of his ethics. To this end, any "commandments" that may be developed with regard to man-and-nature should emphasize responsibility, suggesting what might be "fitting" under various circumstances, more than the identification of specific acts as right or wrong.[7] Man would thus be addressed as a responding being, one who is sensitive to the presence and needs of other beings and feels responsible for the way his actions may affect them. It seems then that our ethic should be not only holistic but situational—with a focus on responsibility.

To illustrate, instead of saying, "You shall not create an imbalance in the ecosystem of nature," it would be better to say, "You shall not do this irresponsibly," i.e., without weighing as many factors as possible and counting the cost, not only to the individuals directly involved but to the whole system. One might be moved to declare, "We simply must not pollute the air." But this would be an impossible stance, for every fire pollutes

---

[7] H. Richard Niebuhr, *The Responsible Self* (New York: Harper & Row, Publishers, 1963), especially Chap. 1.

the air or changes its chemical content to some extent. Yet we must have fires. It is not pollution itself that is wrong, but irresponsible pollution. Likewise, not all killing of animals is evil, but only irresponsible killing. I would be tempted to accept as an absolute the dictum, "Do not crush the spirit of an animal"—in experimentation, or in confinement for exhibition purposes, or by making it unduly dependent upon man (as illustrated in the film "Born Free"). But this too would be indefensible without a specific reference to responsibility.

At this point, a word of caution. Nature is a subject about which it seems easy to be unduly sentimental. It is, of course, quite natural to become emotionally involved with a lovely tree or breathtaking landscape or a primeval wilderness area that is threatened by an industrial development, and to want to protect it fiercely and at all costs—without giving sufficient thought to what those costs may be for the common good. Moreover, it seems all too easy to let one's logic falter with respect to this subject, and to suppose that because life in general is regarded as sacred, all living creatures in particular are to be regarded as sacrosanct and absolutely inviolable.

What is especially unfortunate about this is that it tends to block both heart and mind, and to make almost impossible the kind of judicial thinking that can fairly weigh all conceivable alternatives for action in any given situation. Meaningful distinctions and relativities are lost sight of or explicitly denied, and an oversimplified absolutism takes over. All courses of action are then taken to be either black or white morally, with no intermediate grays. Thus the killing of a mosquito and the killing of a dolphin, or the plucking of a flower and the destruction of a redwood giant, may come to seem equally heinous—or admirable, or inconsequential. And killing for food may seem no better or worse morally than killing for luxury furs; and killing for sport (sheer pleasure or adventure), no different in principle from compassionate mercy killing.

Unselfish love of nature is, however, so legitimate and precious a concern that it must not be allowed to be weakened by association with unfortunate sentimentality or extreme views. This type of concern needs to be conserved or even strengthened wherever it appears, not weakened. I believe this can be done most effectively by relating it rather closely and systematically in our ethical thinking with the idea of responsibility, and by thinking through as specifically as possible just what this may or may not mean in various typical contexts.

4. CORPORATE RESPONSIBILITY

The problems considered thus far represent fairly obvious concerns, and they raise issues that are understood by virtually everybody. We must now face the fact that in our time some of mankind's most serious ethical problems vis-à-vis nature pertain to situations and processes that are so complex that the common man is not equipped to understand them technically. These problems have moral implications of which he is not likely to be aware and for which he must nevertheless, as part of the electorate, bear part of the responsibility in communal policy making. Many of these issues are essentially methodological in kind. They ask not what should be done but how it may be done responsibly. What values must be safeguarded? What tolerances are allowable in regard to safety and quality? What side effects must be taken into account? What price would have to be paid, and would it be justifiable economically or otherwise?

Clearly, whether any given undertaking of this type should be regarded as ethically responsible or irresponsible will depend largely upon technical considerations, about which only experts are competent to make judgments. The common man can himself do little about them directly, aside from participating in general discussion and political action leading to public policy, and to the granting or denying of support for particular projects.

Because of the emergence of such problems—which are the concern of whole populations rather than of individuals and for which the latter can actually bear little direct responsibility—it is important to recognize as a major category of ethical theory the concept of corporate, or explicitly communal, responsibility, as distinguished from personal responsibility. It still seems fashionable to say that ethics and morality are essentially matters of personal responsibility, and that only persons, not communities, can be ultimately concerned and have a conscience. But this will no longer do. Just as mind and spirit are now seen to be functions of both individual organisms and communities of organisms, so ultimate concern, moral sensitivity, and conscience, which are manifestations of mind and spirit, must be recognized as characterizing both individual persons and communities of persons. An adequate contemporary holistic ethic must then be concerned with the development of both a personal and a communal sense of responsibility, and of a fusion of the two.

Just why is this necessary? Take, for instance, the problem of air pollution. What can the individual who is not an expert do about it? He could desist from driving his car and from exhaling tobacco smoke; he could hire experts to clean the smoke that his personally owned factory belches forth, and the like. But actually this might do little more than square himself with his own conscience. As long as others can claim the unilateral right to pollute the air, his own renunciation is of no avail and does little to solve the problem. The problem is regional, not local; and actually it is global and requires a global solution. If Japan were to take all possible antipollution steps, but America would not, the problem would still be unsolved; for the excess carbon dioxide—or whatever—that we would be putting into the air would pollute it over Japan also. All such problems can be solved only by political and diplomatic action, based on a universal shared sense of responsibility and conviction.

In all probability it is here, in this supreme need for a corporate sense of responsibility, especially on a global basis, that man confronts his most formidable problem with regard to his ethical stance toward nature. The technological problems he faces, tough as they will be, will seem as nothing compared to this problem of human relations. How can men of so many radically different cultural backgrounds and personal convictions come to agree—on what is responsible and irresponsible in regard to the very many issues that arise in their dealing with nature—sufficiently to make possible a truly global conscience and ethical commitment? And how can the individual person contribute most effectively to the coming of such a state of affairs? It seems all but impossible, and yet upon that possibility depends the survival of the earth.

III.   TOWARD THE FUTURE

1. SURVIVAL: THE SPACE SHIP

The possibility of a global conscience is, I believe, a very real one. Mankind *will* learn how to achieve a sense of corporate responsibility on a planetary basis—and will learn it within a reasonable time, before it is too late. There is at least one area of general concern in which a worldwide consensus is definitely in the making right now. It pertains to the future of the planet, and arises from the realization that the earth's natural resources will not last forever and that we must *all* join forces in devising systematic efforts to conserve them. We realize, too, that this problem has become acute not simply because the quantity of basic materials is limited but because we have wasted them shamefully; i.e., we have been inexcusably irresponsible in our use and consumption of them.

The sordid story of waste has been told many times and need not be repeated here. Our guilt in this regard is enormous; and let us grant it. The situation *is* very bad. This does not mean, however, that it is beyond repair and hopeless. Nor does it justify the extremely pessimistic forecasts that are so fashionable now regarding the impossibility of the survival of the earth as a place fit for human habitation. The conservation movement is a strong one in many parts of the world, and it has learned a great deal not only about how to protect and conserve but how to repair and reconstruct what has been damaged, and to reclaim or use again what may seem to have been lost.

There was a time early in this century when the situation regarding our forest resources looked very bleak. Millions of acres of forest land had been completely denuded without regard to future needs for wood products and natural beauty. Then, under the leadership of such men as Theodore Roosevelt and Gifford Pinchot, public opinion was aroused and marshalled in support of a great program of conservation control and reforestation, undertaken by both federal and state governments. This has been a magnificent success. With it was developed the science of managing forests in such a way as to assure their continued beauty, hardihood, and growth, while at the same time yielding an ongoing rich harvest of lumber. Today our forests are very extensive; they are said to be quite adequate to meet our foreseeable needs for wood products and to be of much higher quality than the primeval forests ever were. What is especially gratifying is the fact that public opinion has supported the passing and enforcing of strict laws governing the exploitation and protection of forests in terms of truly holistic ecological considerations, taking into account the plant and animal life inhabiting the forests as well as the needs of human beings.

The conservation movement has had other impressive successes that will not be detailed here. The point to be made is that men *can* learn to think and work together on common problems and can develop common ideals and a corporate sense of responsibility. And I believe genuine progress is being made in developing a global determination to save the earth from destruction by the pollution of its atmosphere, waters, and land; to halt the terrible waste of its mineral resources; to keep it from being ruined by overpopulation; and to avoid the horrors of a nuclear explosion holocaust.

There is abroad in the land a powerful symbol, first suggested, I believe, by Adlai Stevenson, and developed by Kenneth Boulding, William Pollard, and others, that has done much to help men sense with desperate urgency how important it is that the earth's materials and energy be conserved and that all men unite in reducing waste.[8,9] It is the symbol of man in an isolated spaceship in which the supply of air and water and of other necessities is definitely limited, and therefore man must use virtually everything over and over again. In such a situation, conservation is indeed a matter of life and death, and that is precisely the situation mankind is in.

With Boulding and others, I realize that man may not learn the art of survival before it is too late. There are many pitfalls he may be unable

---

[8]Kenneth E. Boulding, *The Meaning of the Twentieth Century* (New York: Harper & Row, Publishers, Colophon Books, 1964).

[9]William G. Pollard, *Man On a Spaceship* (Claremont, Calif.: Claremont Colleges, 1967).

to avoid. However, there are good reasons to believe that man can and will avoid them, and that he and his world will survive.

2. MORE THAN SURVIVAL: A "NEW EARTH"

Despite what has just been said, I submit that the most important question before us is not, after all, whether global catastrophe can be avoided but what man will do with the earth if he does survive. It would be a great pity, therefore, if man's concerns about the future of the earth were dominated exclusively by a crisis psychology of fear. To be sure, conserving its resources and protecting it from human despoliation are extremely important; but so also are its improvement and further development.

In what sense does it need improving? In the first place, although the earth *is* a systemic whole, it is still in the making, incomplete and far from perfect. As Pollard has said so eloquently in his chapter, our planet is a beautiful and precious gem, and we should cherish it. It is not, however, a flawless gem; in fact it has some downright abominable features that man, if he survives, should endeavor to eliminate rather than to conserve. Thus there are disease-carrying rats that attack babies in their cribs, yellow-fever mosquitoes, ticks and tsetse flies, cockroaches, and myriads of other kinds of vermin that seem to serve no useful purpose whatsoever but simply make existence miserable for both man and beast. There are also the various cancers—life gone berserk. Then, too, there are the hurricanes, earthquakes, avalanches, tidal waves, and conflagrations. And not the least deplorable aspect of nature is the lethal savagery of man. The world would be better off without all of these.

Man's elimination of these features, of course, would constitute deliberate intervention in nature, an uprooting and destruction of what nature has brought forth, a rupturing of relationships in it, and an excising of realities from the systemic whole. Wouldn't this violate a basic principle of the ethic being advocated here? No, it wouldn't. Nowhere have I said that *all* nature's realities and relationships are sacred and not to be tampered with. My position has been that none should be tampered with *irresponsibly*, and that "those decisions and actions that bring about maximization of such interrelation and interdependence as make for wholeness should be designated as morally responsible and right. . . ."

Rats and cockroaches in slum areas, tsetse flies in Africa, malignant cancer in a man or animal, a hurricane in the Caribbean, human savagery anywhere—none of these factors makes for wholeness or mutuality. So far as I can see there is nothing good or sacred about them; they are demonic and destructive of unity. Hence a holistic ethic must proscribe them, and it must demand their minimization and even their elimination whenever possible. The injunction to love nature rests not primarily on its absolute loveliness but upon its need to be loved—precisely because it is not lovely in many ways, but by being loved can become so. Reverence for life and love of nature call for vigorous remedial treatment, not for a hands-off policy.

Now one of the most admirable—and most fundamental—features of nature is that it is not fixed in its qualitative attributes, so that betterment is possible not only by excision of the undesirable but by development through transformation and creation of novelty that enhances the good. I take this dynamism and developmental creativity of nature to be among the most basic and sacral realities of the cosmos, and conclude, therefore, that it is part of man's responsibility to use his power in such a manner as to be consistent with, and supportive of, that cosmic creativity.

In this regard, the symbol of man in a spaceship is inadequate. It does not bring into bold relief the dynamic features of the world and the importance of creative endeavor on the part of man. Another symbol seems to me to be much more helpful, namely, the ancient symbol of the fertile garden and its husbandman who is at once its conservator-protector-pathologist and developer. I suggest that the sense of responsibility that this imagery evokes imputes greater importance to the second of these functions—that of developer—especially when it is contemplated in the light of yet another ancient symbol, that of the "new earth." For it conceives the task to be futurist in purpose in accord with the futurist drives of the garden.

This symbolism has often been given otherworldly interpretations, especially when prevailing cosmological concepts made the idea of a new earth unthinkable except by trans-natural means. Now, however, a radically transformed earth is widely regarded as not only possible but highly probable. It seems to me therefore that man's ethical stance toward nature should be consciously and responsibly future-oriented, looking forward courageously and expectantly to a greatly transformed new earth, to the coming of which he should be anxious to contribute mightily. This would label as irresponsible the attitude that steels itself against the future and instinctively regards all danger and risk as something to be shunned, yielding to change only reluctantly and as though "safety first" were an ethical absolute.

What kinds of radical changes should be regarded as desirable "advances" and "for the better"? Those, I suggest, that enhance the systemic wholeness of the earth by strengthening and/or increasing the interdependency, mutuality, and communality of all its worthy inhabitants, both human and nonhuman. Negatively speaking, getting rid of unworthy vermin, malignancies, and cataclysms would count as advances. More positively, there would be a great advance if our systems of transportation and communication could be made truly worldwide to assure prompt sharing globally of all desirable experience and goods and to promote a high standard of living everywhere. To this end many new materials will be needed both as components of the distribution system and as goods to be shared. To meet new needs, many of the new materials will have to exhibit physical properties that do not exist now, so that they must be created *de novo*, just as the synthetic plastics were. Thus in the new earth there will be new foods, new clothing, new shelters, new drugs, new machines, and much else that comes under the heading of material things. And let it be noted that we are talking about *nature* itself and its newness, for nature will contain new molecules and new forces among them, and new structural combinations of them—all new creations. Nor is it inconceivable that in the future there may be in the atmosphere, in the ocean, and in the lithosphere of the earth potent new relationships that would take the curse from the hurricane and earthquake. The whole ecosystem of the earth may be significantly different because of these novelties.

Other new creations are in the offing also, such as new biological entities: new seeds and plants; new eggs, embryos, and animals; and perhaps new forms of life itself—forms that are generated "artificially" in the laboratory and follow a different evolutionary path than has been known thus far. Even the minds of men and animals may be greatly modified or changed. All this too is nature, and not in any sense beyond nature. It means that within nature itself there will be new physiological and psychological realities and new causal relationships. More concretely, it means that there will be significantly different animal and human bodies-and-psyches, which will perhaps be more resistant to physical and mental disease, able to reason more easily, remember better, be more stable emotionally, develop different behavior patterns, and be ethically more responsible.

I am keenly aware that the preceding paragraph has led me rather far into what many people would say is sheer speculation—irresponsible Utopian dreaming. But I would plead otherwise. It is indisputable that, returning to the symbol of the garden, its gardener has recently entered into a new relationship with it. He has taken a hand in its evolutionary development and has become the creator of many new realities within it. For a century and a half now he has been making changes in its landscaping, its physical aspects, and thus in the environment of its inhabitants. During recent decades, however, he has begun to modify it drastically at its very foundation levels, those of the molecule, the living cell, and the mind and spirit. And there have been quite enough of such achievements under experimental control conditions to provide ample reason for expecting many more in the future. Although the prediction of specific details is admittedly still unreliable, that of general possibilities is not.

Let us note especially that the earth will be new not only because it will contain many novelties but because the systemic relationship between garden (nature) and gardener (man) will be truly new. Until recently the earth was a dual system, the gardener thinking of himself as separate from the garden and operating upon it from the outside. Now he realizes that he is an integral part of nature, operating within it. Moreover he has discovered that he can therein wield creative power formerly attributed to God only. At the same time he has found that nature is itself creative, according to the pattern of emergent evolution, and that he is profoundly affected by it and even dependent upon it for his humanity.

There are, of course, tremendous risks in man's trying to shape the future of the world and of himself. What I have anticipated as "advance" and "for the better" may turn out to be exactly the opposite. Nevertheless, I would plead that it would be inexcusably and tragically irresponsible of man not to enter this area of creative endeavor.

3. The Counterculture: Radiance and Mystery

Not long ago some of our best students attended classes in high school and in university with flowers and bells. They were part of a strong movement toward what is being called the counterculture. This movement is devoted to bringing about a new earth. Its main concern, however, touches upon certain aspects of reality about which I have said virtually nothing explicitly, namely those dimensions and qualities of existence that lie outside of the purview of science proper—those that Alfred North Whitehead was thinking about when he said:

> When you understand all about the sun and all about the atmosphere and all about the rotation of the earth, you may still miss the radiance of the sunset.[10]

The movement feels that contemporary scholarship, including religion, has allowed the "radiance" features of nature—its charm that enchants men, and its mystery that awes them and causes them to wonder—to be eclipsed too much by the material features. And our youth with

---

[10]Alfred North Whitehead, *Science and the Modern World* (New York: The Macmillan Company, 1926), p. 286.

flowers and bells claim that contemporary education has extolled too much the virtues of the objective, rational, and rigorous, while derogating utterly the subjective, nonrational, and intuitive. They feel that life is being dehumanized in this way, and they blame science and technology for this sad state of affairs. They also deplore the polluting and defacing of the earth, but they regard this as heinous not for the usual and more materialistic reasons but for the more subtle one that dirt and filth and ugliness choke off radiance and stifle the sense of wonder and awe. Will the "new earth," they are asking, be a world of enchantment or disenchantment? And to assure the former, rather than the latter, they are driving toward a counterculture, one that will repudiate the materialism of the present culture.

One of the movement's most sensitive and eloquent interpreters is Theodore Roszak, who has issued the following manifesto, with the substance of which I agree fully.

> This . . . is the primary project of our counter culture: to proclaim *a new heaven and a new earth* so vast, so marvelous that the *inordinate* claims of technical expertise must of necessity withdraw in the presence of such splendor to a subordinate and marginal status in the lives of men. To create and broadcast such a consciousness of life entails nothing less than the willingness to open ourselves to the visionary imagination on its own demanding terms. We must be prepared to entertain the astonishing claim . . . that here are eyes which see the world not (only) as commonplace sight or scientific scrutiny sees it, but see it transformed, made lustrous beyond measure, and in seeing the world so, see it as it really is (and will be).[11]

I would plead, however, that it is only the unreasonable and inordinate claims of technical expertise that will have to withdraw in the presence of the new vision—not the sensible, profound ones that characterize science and technology at their best.

The truth is that the science of today is in many ways very different from that of the nineteenth and early twentieth century—witness the remarkable new antimaterialistic insights about the basic character of physical reality and of nature, insights that have been cited as the conceptual foundation for this chapter. These new understandings and the new attitudes toward nature that accompany them tend to enrich and amplify—rather than impoverish—man's experience of radiance and mystery. Furthermore, their conceptual meaning is increased tremendously

---

[11]Theodore Roszak, *The Making of a Counter Culture* (Garden City, N.Y.: Doubleday & Company, Inc., Anchor Books, 1969), p. 240. (With apologies to Roszak, italics and parentheses added.)

when it is coupled with that of process thought (see following section), which provides a world view that is friendly rather than inimical to ideas of radiance and mystery.

Thus the ethical stance being advocated here finds additional support in the growing awareness that the wonder-evoking qualities of radiance and mystery constitute fundamental realities of nature, realities that man should regard as sacred and which should be conserved and enhanced as he plans and builds the "new earth" of the future. It must not be a world of disenchantment—and the most compelling reason is that the earth is the Lord's.

4. THE LORD'S

But why drag in God? Isn't the beautiful ecosystem that we have been considering self-sufficient? And hasn't man come of age in it, so that he no longer needs God? Thus far in my discussion of an ethical stance toward nature very little has actually been said about God. Even mention of the first great commandment—to love God—was rather casual, and no particular reason was given for its inclusion. Why then talk about "the Lord" now?

The reason is that the imagery of the garden does include the figure of God, for whom the gardener acts as steward-caretaker of the garden and to whom he is responsible. There is much wisdom in this and tremendous motivating power. And I have come to feel strongly that no other motivation—such as a sense of responsibility to fellow man or to nature—can of itself provide the degree of motivational support that is necessary to attain and maintain the sort of ethical stance toward nature that is needed in our time and in the future. This is why in our Western religious tradition (the Hebrew-Christian tradition) the first basic principle of the moral life is taken to be *love of God*, for it is out of *love of God* that the sense of *responsibility to God* emerges. Not only, however, is this a matter of feeling or sensing responsibility; it is rather that the rich imagery of *the garden and its husbandman and their God* symbolizes a powerful conceptuality that is indispensable to the adequacy of ethical thinking and theory. In other words, I suggest that the vocabulary of ethics must include the term God or its equivalent.

It is important to recognize that for many men—of many religions— nature is sacramental; it is experienced as a visible reality through which the presence of the invisible God becomes real in their lives. For them this is the supreme mystery of nature, that through its finitudes and immediacies men somehow become aware of ultimacy, and that despite its many dark opacities and imperfections, it yet transmits to them the light and glory and love of God.

Unfortunately for many people and for quite some time, this kind of talk about God has been largely meaningless. In part this is because the term God has all too often been defined and interpreted philosophically and theologically in terms of ideas that are no longer tenable today, for instance, ideas from thoroughly outmoded cosmologies. I feel, however, that the new understandings of science presented above, combined with those of process thought, are radically altering the situation, so that the idea of God is again becoming truly meaningful—both philosophically and religiously.

According to this view the world is much more like a living organism or society or process than an inanimate machine. Its most fundamental components are relationships and events. In it life, mind, and spirit are natural qualities or states of physical reality, not ethereal essences exported into nature from a supra-natural realm. The world is developmental, and it is still becoming. In this system, subjective aims are causal, as truly as are physical forces. All objects and occasions have such aims, which in part determine their future. They also are endowed with the freedom or capacity to choose among various possibilities represented by those aims. Thus the forces of the universe are more persuasive than coercive.

Religiously speaking, God is the redeemer-creator who is at work among men, giving them faith and strength for their life and work. Metaphysically speaking, God is the supreme exemplification of the basic principles of the universe, e.g., of relationality, mutuality, responsiveness, and of creativity. He is a full-fledged member of the community of beings that make up the world. He is the great giver—of aims and possibilities; and the great persuader—who with those aims lures beings into the future. He both moves and is moved by all living things, and is therefore the great coparticipant in all of life, the supreme risk taker, sufferer, and conqueror of adversity. He is the great cocreator who shares his creativity with his creations, and they join him in determining the future. His supreme power is love, and this also he shares. He is immanent in the world, though also transcendent to it.

This thought recognizes that man has come of age and does not need a *deus ex machina,* or a god of the gaps who is outside of the world and intervenes in it coercively to achieve extra-natural events. It does not agree, however, that man can therefore be said to get along without God, for it conceives God to be integrally a participant in the world, immanently and inseparably at the heart of every object and occasion, making it possible for all things to exist and to respond or not to respond to the lures he places before them. Thus no man is independent of God, though he may not realize it. To love God is to respond to his love and to align oneself with his freely offered aims for one's own life and for the world.

It means joining him in his creative and redemptive acts of love. It means being aware of his intimate and loving presence in all occasions, and having a sense of responsibility to him for what one does on all occasions. There can be no more potent a foundation for an ethic of decision making with regard to nature—or anything else. Only thus can there be true love of both neighbor and nature. And only thus can the "new earth" be a good earth, one that will not have lost its enchantment and in which all men can be truly human—and all other beings fully themselves. It is because these are very real possibilities—and not at all mere wishful dreams—that we can say confidently that the earth is indeed the Lord's.

HAROLD K. SCHILLING was trained as a physicist and has spent much of his career at Pennsylvania State University, where he has been successively Chairman of the Physics Department, Dean of the Graduate School, and University Professor. His book Science and Religion: An Interpretation of Two Communities *is a study of methodological problems in the two fields. He is coauthor of* Teacher Education and Religion. *Several of his articles have explored relationships between science and religion.*

ROGER L. SHINN

8

Science and
Ethical Decision
some new issues

Modern man, long accustomed to seeing science as a benefactor, is rather suddenly asking whether it is a menace. Scientists themselves are increasingly perplexed by the social consequences of their achievements. Once they were inclined to consider the value of scientific endeavor to be self-authenticating. Now they wonder whether mankind is capable of coping with the scientific power let loose in the world.

When C. P. Snow wrote his book, *The Two Cultures and the Scientific Revolution*, in 1959, he found one of the marks of the scientific-technological culture to be a basic optimism about man's social condition. The scientist was habituated to progress. He was trained in problem solving. Where others indulged in despair over human ineptitude and misery, scientists located a problem and went to work on it. The second culture, the literary-intellectual, was likely to criticize the scientific culture for its shallow optimism, according to Snow. This second culture reveled in existentialist *angst* and indulged in dismal forebodings about man and his future.

Although anybody could think of exceptions, Snow's characterizations held up rather well at the time. But a startling change of mood has since stirred the scientific community. There is today an apocalyptic anxiety among scientists. I do not claim that all scientists share in the mood, but I do maintain that the language of apocalypse is currently more often heard among scientists than among theologians. The American Museum of Natural History entitled its centennial exhibit, "Can Man Survive?" Recent meetings of the American Association for the Advancement of Science have produced a rash of headlines warning humanity of impending doom, and the organization's publication, *Science*, has often returned to the theme. To take a single example, not uncharacteristic, John Platt, a research biophysicist and associate director of the University of Michigan Mental Health Research Institute, warns mankind of "a shorter life expectancy than people have ever had in the world before." He estimates, "We may have even less than a 50–50 chance of living until 1980."[1]

If we look for the reasons for the change, we find them in society's shifting awareness of two characteristics of science. The first is the ability of science to solve problems. The second is the tendency of science and the technology derived from it to make and intensify problems.

Science as a problem solver has increased human opportunities. It has reduced the scourges of poverty and disease. It has relieved man of much drudgery and has multiplied human powers so that a person, whose brute strength is insignificant, can by touching a switch command thousands of horsepower. It has even "solved" some ethical problems, or removed them from the common life; for instance, the sharing of food in times of famine, a perennial ethical problem, ceases to be a problem in technological societies that never experience famine. Even more impressive to many has been the scientific method—nondogmatic, exploratory, open to new truth, ready to subject every belief to procedures for verification. A sizable portion of modern man has been ready to join John Dewey in his rhapsodic paraphrase of the biblical Book of Job: "Though this method slay my most cherished belief, yet will I trust it."[2]

Society likes to turn ethical problems into technical problems, ideological clashes into pragmatic inquiries, basic human conflicts into questions of know-how. Hence society may be unprepared when pragmatic success and know-how betray it by precipitating new ethical agonies, or when science and technology, although solving some problems, produce new problems and expand some old ones. The most obvious example is weaponry. I am not here assigning moral blame to science. It is people, not science, who use weapons; but because of scientific technology they can use weapons with more frightening damage than in any prescientific time. In countless other ways a technological society heightens the deliberate and the unconscious destructive powers of man. Albert Szent-Gyorgyi, biochemist and Nobel laureate in medicine, writes: "Science,

---

[1] John Platt, "What We Must Do," *Science*, 166 (November 28, 1969), 1116.
[2] John Dewey, "Fundamentals," *New Republic*, 37 (1924), 276.

with the powerful tools it gave us, made us outgrow our little globe. We can foul it, bury it in garbage, make cesspools out of the oceans, exhaust our resources and wipe ourselves out."[3] Today, as a result, there are many who fear science-technology and even demonize it. As Alvin M. Weinberg, Director of the Oak Ridge National Laboratory, has written: "Science and its technologies are today on the defensive," and the attack "is most notice-able in the United States"[4]—the country, it might be added, that once glorified technology more than any other. Theodore Roszak has pointed out that the really novel quality in youthful radicalism today, as compared with radicalism of previous generations, is "that a radical rejection of science and technological values should appear so close to the center of our society."[5]

In this historical setting I wish to set forth three propositions. (1) Scientific-technological advance presents man with decisions that are not simply scientific but are ethical and political. (2) Scientists and technologists have a peculiar moral responsibility in the world they so powerfully shape. (3) Scientific-technological transformation requires revision of religious-theological-ethical traditions.

Before elaborating these propositions, I should make a comment on vocabulary. In referring to science and technology, scientific technology, and scientific-technological advance, I have avoided the subtle questions of the relation between science and technology. Clearly the two are not the same. Pure science may be utterly indifferent to technology, as it often was among the ancient Greeks. Technology, concerned to get "more bang for a buck" and more gross national product for less work, may be hostile to the theoretical and aesthetic motivations of pure science. Nevertheless, the dominating characteristic of this technological epoch has been the wedding of science and technology. The elaborate technologies of today are utterly dependent upon science—sometimes a science deliberately commissioned by government or industry to get results, sometimes a pure science that by serendipity produces technological results. Conversely, science is increasingly dependent upon technology. Lord Rutherford (1871–1937) is sometimes said to have been the last great scientist who did physics with a straightedge, a ball of sealing wax, and a piece of string. Scientists who use cyclotrons and lasers know their dependence upon technicians. As physicist Victor Weisskopf points out, scientific dis-

---

[3]Albert Szent-Gyorgyi, "15 Minutes to Zero," *New York Times*, September 15, 1970.
[4]Alvin M. Weinberg, "In Defense of Science," *Science*, 167 (January 9, 1970), 141.
[5]Theodore Roszak, *The Making of a Counter Culture* (Garden City, N.Y.: Doubleday & Company, Inc., Anchor Books, 1969), p. 51.

coveries often have to wait for the technological development that makes them possible.[6] It is therefore the combination of science and technology that is the subject of my three propositions.

I. FROM SCIENCE TO ETHICS TO POLITICS

Scientific technology, presenting mankind with new possibilities for the enhancement or destruction of life, requires society to make ethical decisions. Whereas individuals may decide about their own personal acts, decisions on the social level are made through political processes in which scientists may participate but are not likely to have the decisive word.

The most obvious example, already mentioned, is weaponry. Only a highly theoretical science combined with a sophisticated technology can produce nuclear and thermonuclear weapons systems. Whether such systems are the best use of science is not itself a scientific issue. Questions about the destruction of life are basically ethical questions, now raised to an enormity never known in past history. They weigh on the consciences of many individuals who must decide whether to enter military service, whether to design and build weapons, or whether to do basic research that may contribute to the arts of war. Some individuals decide that they will, as far as possible, renounce the system and withdraw from participation; but they know that others will participate. The basic decisions about the assignment of priorities for research and for military production and about the use of weapons are political decisions. The scientist who makes possible a new kind of destruction may, like Albert Einstein find himself helpless to influence its outcome.

This movement of the focus of an issue from science to ethics to politics, so evident in matters of war and peace, is a pattern often repeated and likely to become increasingly prevalent in our world. Three cases in point present the issue: population, ecology, and genetics.

The population explosion, although it crept up on a largely unaware world, has by this time pretty well impressed itself upon the consciousness of most highly educated societies. There is no need to pile up the data here; a few examples will suffice. The world's population is growing at a rate that doubles the total in about 35 years. Although it required all human history (perhaps a million years) up to 1850 for man's numbers to reach one billion, the human race now adds a billion in less than 15

---

[6]Victor F. Weisskopf, *Knowledge and Wonder*, rev. ed. (Garden City, N.Y.: Doubleday & Company, Inc., Anchor Books, 1966), pp. 107–108. Cf. Jacques Ellul, *The Technological Society* (New York: Random House, Inc., Vintage Books), 1964, pp. 7–10.

years. A continuation of the present rate of growth would mean that in 600 years there would be a person for every square yard of land, including the surface of Antarctica, the Sahara desert, and Mount Everest. If this is not frightening enough, the projection can be continued until—to state the mathematically accurate but physically impossible consequence— people would outweigh the earth, the solar system, and eventually the known universe. Obviously the process will stop, but it is not yet obvious what will stop it.

The population crisis is largely a crisis caused by science. Prescientific societies often had their local population problems, which were at least partially solved by exposure of infants and the aged or by conquest of their neighbors. Today, however, the problem has expanded on a world scale, resulting from scientific achievements in overcoming disease and famine. Science also has furnished remedies for overpopulation (notably, contraception), provided people choose to use them, but individual choice is not the only force at work. Social policy, set by inherently political processes, has become increasingly important.

In most major nations the government is now doing something, timidly or aggressively, about population. As the squeeze gets tighter (to use a metaphor whose literal meaning is increasingly applicable), the government will be forced to augment its activity. Men will face again the age-old ethical problem of how to relate personal freedom to social good. The procreative acts of men and women have often been regarded as intimately personal; yet when procreation becomes a social menace, society has a stake in these personal decisions. Paul Ehrlich asks why people are willing to fight coercive wars, yet are squeamish about coercion in population policy.[7] Even more emphatically, Garrett Hardin argues: "To couple the concept of freedom to breed with the belief that everyone born has an equal right to the commons [the world's food and other resources] is to lock the world into a tragic course of action."[8]

Actually the decision will not be a clear-cut choice between total freedom to procreate and total coercion. A great variety of social incentives, many of them simply extensions of present policies, will operate. Policies regarding taxation, availability of housing, and educational opportunities for children will come into play increasingly. Such governmental policies will influence personal choices. The policies will be determined politically as an outcome of the values, interests, and pressures at work in the society. We do not yet know whether the result will move toward justice or injustice. We can expect strenuous conflicts of interest. The black

[7]Paul Ehrlich, *The Population Bomb* (New York: Ballantine Books, Inc., 1968), p. 166.
[8]Garrett Hardin, "The Tragedy of the Commons," *Science*, 152 (December 13, 1968), 1243–48. Reprinted in *The Environmental Handbook*, ed. Garrett De Bell (New York: Ballantine Books, Inc., 1970).

community, for example, is mistrustful of all proposals that put pressure on its members to reduce their reproduction. (At the First National Congress on Optimum Population and Environment in 1970 the black caucus walked out in protest against "oppression of individual freedom," with explicit reference to Garrett Hardin's arguments that voluntarism would not be adequate.) The black distrust of white manipulation is based on long experience. It points to the inescapable fact that when scientific change requires revision of public policies, the determination of the policies is primarily a political rather than a scientific act.

A second problem area, partly a consequence of population, is ecology, which "may indeed constitute the most dangerous and difficult challenge that humanity has ever faced."[9] The more people there are, the more they threaten their environment. But more important than sheer numbers are patterns of consumption. People who eat large quantities of meat and live in air-conditioned buildings consume the earth's resources at a far greater rate than people who eat mostly grains and live in mud huts. People who travel by automobile and airplane foul the atmosphere more malignantly than people who walk. Thus far in modern history, affluence and the ecological crisis have advanced together. It is possible that men less careless and less greedy might develop a high standard of living less ecologically destructive than that of North America.

There is no need here to collect horror stories, of which there are plenty, on the ecological crisis. A few examples will make the point that an ecologically destructive use of technology requires ethical and political solutions. (a) Every city in the United States is perplexed by what to do with waste. The average person in this country discards 5.3 pounds of solid waste per day, almost a ton a year, and the rate is rising. (b) Likewise every city is haunted with problems of pollution, caused largely by the automobile and industrial atmospheric wastes. From 25,000 miles in space the astronauts could see Los Angeles as a filthy smudge on California's coast. The problem is getting worse. Rising population and rising standards of consumption steadily increase the number of cars, and most metropolitan areas anticipate a doubled consumption of electrical power over the next decade, while utilities and conservationists fight over the location of new power plants. (c) Rivers and lakes get more loaded with human and industrial wastes. The situation becomes ridiculous when a river, as happened to Cleveland's Cuyahoga, catches fire and burns two bridges. The pollution of Lake Erie has gone so far that even if all pollution were to stop now, a restoration of the relative purity of 25 years ago would require an estimated $40 billion and 50–500 years.[10] (d) On a

[9]Robert Heilbroner, New York Review of Books, April 23, 1970, p. 3.
[10]Robert Humphries, "The Imperiled Environment," Vista, 5, No. 5 (March–April 1970), 18.

vast scale, mankind is consuming oxygen and producing carbon dioxide, meanwhile reducing the earth's green areas and fouling the oceans that reverse the process. A possible consequence is the "greenhouse affect," raising the earth's temperature with the consequence of melting the polar icecaps and changing the configuration of the seashores. No one is sure that this will happen or at what moment such a process may become irreversible; but mankind simply goes its way, not stopping to reckon the consequences.

In this grab bag of examples one common element is clear. In no case will a few acts of restraint by conscientious people make very much difference. Only a large-scale social policy is adequate. Technology, which has contributed to the problem, can help solve it through new techniques of reclaiming wastes and recycling valuable raw materials. But there is little incentive for any individual or industrial firm to accept the cost of such methods in the face of competitors who do not. The political answer may come in a form of social cost accounting that reckons and assigns to industry the costs of damage to the environment. For a factory to pollute a stream rather than cleanse its waste products is cheaper for the industrial unit but is socially expensive. Social cost accounting would modify motivations and practices.

The whole problem becomes incredibly difficult on an international scale. For example, the United States, with 6 percent of the world's population, consumes about 40 percent of the world's raw materials. Some estimates run as high as 50 percent.[11] The United States contributes a comparable amount of the world's pollution. It is obviously impossible within any foreseeable future for the world to step up its consumption and pollution to the rate of the United States. On the other hand, it is just as unlikely, barring catastrophe, that the United States would reduce its rates to the world's level. The affluent and powerful nations, precisely because they are affluent and powerful, will resist any international accountability.

In both national and international cases it becomes evident that a technological situation requires decisions that are both ethical and political. And political answers by their very nature involve conflicts of interest and the play of power rather than the dispassionate workings of scientific reason. Such a judgment sometimes comes from the center of the scientific establishment. Thus W. D. McElroy, Director of the National Science Foundation, in responding to the forebodings of John Platt (quoted earlier), writes: "The most serious problems listed present a common feature: they will be settled principally by political decision, by economic

---

[11] I am using the more modest figure, as did Robert S. McNamara, President of the World Bank, in an address to the Board of Governors. See the *New York Times*, September 29, 1970.

choice, and by the education of people."[12] I might add that education will have little effect except as it influences economic and political decisions.

The third problem arises from increased scientific understanding of genetics. It is often discussed in the context of the population issue. Demographers are likely to advocate acceptance of the standard of the two-child family as a maximum. At this point some geneticists quickly say that some families should have more than two children whereas others should have fewer or none. Their concern is for minimizing undesirable genetic "loads" (negative eugenics) and maximizing desirable heredity (positive eugenics). Immediately the question arises as to who will have the right to determine what is good and bad heredity and to decide which families shall be encouraged to have children and which ones discouraged.

The issue becomes magnified by the consideration of further genetic possibilities. One of these is the establishment of sperm banks to be used for artificial insemination. The late Herman J. Muller, a renowned geneticist, proposed that the sperm of great men be maintained in frozen form for many years and be made available for the fathering of children by many mothers. This proposal is generally considered to be technically feasible. A further step would involve the transplanting of ova, so that a woman might bear a child whose genetic makeup was the product of a male and female chosen for presumably desirable inheritable qualities. Another possibility is the use of various mechanical and chemical devices for the selection and modification of genes so as to improve the heredity of future generations of children. Determination of the sex of future children appears to be imminently feasible; on the other hand, the making of children to order remains thus far in the realm of science fiction, and many geneticists think it will remain there for the foreseeable future. But between the steps that are early probabilities and those that are more remote are a variety on which geneticists disagree as to feasibility.

All these possibilities, both the probable and the improbable, raise the same wider issues we have seen in the case of population and ecology. Science opens up new capabilities, but science does not itself determine their use. Among some geneticists there is a strong conviction that they know what the ideal human types are and therefore the world should gladly follow their advice. Other geneticists are much more modest in their claims and much more aware of the pretensions involved in ordaining the future heredity of men. Theodosius Dobzhansky has asked the critical question:

> Are we to have, in place of Plato's philosopher-king, a geneticist king? And who will be president of the National Sperm Bank and of the National

---

[12]"A Crisis of Crises," *Science*, 167 (January 2, 1970), 9, editorial.

DNA Bank? What checks and balances are to be imposed on the genetic legislature and the genetic executive powers? Who will guard the guardians?[13]

A little imagination suggests some fantastic scenarios in case genetic manipulation becomes practical. For example, will the United States, Russia, and China (if these are still dominant world powers by that time) engage in a genetics race, comparable to the armaments races of today? If so, will their aim be to produce a breed of magnificent warriors? And will some small power protest in the United Nations that the world does not need superior warriors—with perhaps as much effect as the small powers now protest that the world does not need more nuclear weapons? Will some geneticist, worried about what a prospective enemy is doing, volunteer information to our government and then live to regret the use that is made of it, as Einstein did in the case of the atomic bomb? Will race prejudice in high places operate designedly or subconsciously to perpetuate some racial types and eliminate others?

It may be that all these questions are fantastic because they are based on exaggerated expectations of progress in eugenic science. But much of the science fiction of the past is prosaic fact today, and in any event the issues arise in even the more modest genetic steps that are already realizable or imminent. The argument came to an interesting focus in December of 1969 at a conference on theology and the life sciences, cosponsored by the Boston University School of Theology and the American Association for the Advancement of Science. Dr. Bernard Davis of the Harvard Medical School presented a paper, temperate by comparison with some of the more ambitious proposals of geneticists, in which he argued that modern life had developed in such complexity that people of quite low intelligence simply could not cope with it. Sooner or later, he proposed, steps would be needed to prevent the birth of children with very low inherited intelligence. The paper was more modest than those of many geneticists, because it acknowledged that we do not now have adequate devices for measuring innate intelligence in isolation from the cultural components that enter into personality. In addition, Dr. Davis offered warnings against misuses of the proposed program.

Even so, the paper provoked a biting reply. One young man "demanded" an opportunity to reply. He was Dr. James Shapiro, who a month earlier had earned international fame as part of the team of Harvard scientists who for the first time isolated a gene. Shapiro, in a dramatic renunciation of his own achievement and future scientific career, argued that our present society can make only evil uses of scientific attainments

[13]"Changing Man," *Science*, 155 (January 27, 1967), 413.

and that scientists should stop their research. So long as men like Nixon and Agnew determine the directions of society, he argued, scientists should stop producing the knowledge that politics will misuse.[14]

In the discussion that followed, some scientists pointed out that suspension of genetic research would be in effect a suspension of cancer research, since the same basic science of the biological cell underlies both. Shapiros reply was to accept the premise and recommend that elimination of pollution, smoking, and food additives be substituted for cancer research.

Not all who were present accepted Shapiro's "New Left" style or his specific choice of political symbols. Even fewer accepted the anti-intellectualism implicit in his rejection of basic scientific research.[15] But everyone understood in some degree his contention that science does not control its own consequences, that the political process in large measure decrees the uses of science, and that even the scientist when he projects social goals is likely to project his own cultural prejudices. The last point in particular received reinforcement later in the day when one enthusiast for genetics, in a discussion of the planned heredity of future generations, dropped the remark that the human race cannot afford another Dostoevski.

On rare occasions some scientist wonders aloud whether there should be a moratorium on scientific research until mankind can think through the purposes for which it wants to use science. Dr. James F. Danielli, leader of the team that produced an amoeba out of constituents from several other amoebas, has urged the creation of a national or international agency to police scientific research and safeguard mankind from its disastrous possibilities.[16] Many scientists look upon such heresy with the furious anger that the Inquisition directed at unitarianism. However, the threat of political intrusion upon scientific research is real. For example, in the United States politics already dictates in large part the direction of

---

[14]Dr. Shapiro was not a loner within the team on which he worked to isolate the gene. Dr. Jon Beckwith, the leader of the team, had earlier told the press: "It becomes more and more frightening—especially when we see work in biology used by our government in Vietnam and in devising chemical and biological weapons" (*New York Times*, November 23, 1969).

[15]The argument subsequently continued in a wider forum. Shapiro's position was reported in an interview, "Harvard Genetics Researcher Quits Science for Politics," *Science*, 167 (February 13, 1970), 963–64. Shapiro was supported to some extent by Salvador E. Luria, geneticist at the Massachusetts Institute of Technology and cowinner of the Nobel award for physiology or medicine of 1969. Shapiro was attacked by a group of scientists for raising "the specter of fear of science" as did the persecutors of Socrates and Galileo, and the modern forces that destroyed Soviet genetics and German biochemistry and physics (see *Science*, 167 (March 27, 1970), 1668).

[16]Reported by Walter Sullivan in the *New York Times*, December 8, 1970.

scientific energies when, out of $26 billion going into research and development, $17 billion comes from the federal government, including $14 billion from the Defense Department, the Atomic Energy Commission, and the National Aeronautics and Space Administration.[17] The contemporary problem is not totally new, although its dimensions are radically new. Every advance in knowledge and power since the dawn of history has heightened man's creative and destructive powers. The inventers of the wheel and the lever could no more determine what would be done with wheels and levers than could Einstein determine what the Pentagon would do with nuclear energy, or can Shapiro determine what will become of his research on the gene. The faith that knowledge is good, that the conquest of ignorance is a gain, that increased understanding and power are desirable—all these are articles of faith, not strictly verifiable except within the faith system. At that point, science and theology are comparable disciplines. Both live by faith, and their styles of faith have their hazards as well as their promises.

II. SCIENCE AND ETHICAL RESPONSIBILITY

Power implies responsibility. Science and technology, as the sources of immense power, are therefore the inheritors of an ethical responsibility. Whether eagerly or reluctantly, scientists increasingly feel this burden. In describing it, I want to reject two common simplifications of the situation.

The first is the expectation that a scientific elite can decide what is good for the whole society. Such a stance is pretentious if assumed by scientists, escapist if adopted by the rest of society. In ethical decisions, everybody has responsibility. In setting social policies, the entire society has the right and responsibility to participate in the decisions. On many an issue society needs the illumination that comes via the poet, the artist, the prophet, and the saint. If the scientist has a peculiar awareness of the consequences of his achievements, the beneficiaries and victims of those achievements have their awareness too. Thus the economist, the architect, and the medical investigator have knowledge that is hidden from most people. Yet the poor man has an economic experience unknown to the brilliant economist; for example, people in housing projects discover some things that architects apparently don't know, and suffering patients feel the pains of sickness (both physical and economic) in a way that healthy and affluent medical researchers do not. Ethical sensitivity is not identical

---

[17]The figures are reported by Stephen Solomon, "Chained Campuses," *New Republic*, September 19, 1970, p. 12.

with scientific competence, even though the two qualities sometimes happily coincide. Many a scientist in our time has forcefully refuted the efforts of those who, impressed by his achievements, want to ascribe to him a mistaken authority in human affairs.

The opposite simplification declares, in an excessive scientific detachment and innocence, that science has no responsibility for the consequences of its activities. The scientist, according to this line, simply does his job, motivated by a sheer desire to enlarge knowledge. The scientific quest is a good, perhaps even sacred, calling—the scientist has no responsibility for the uses to which other men may put his discoveries. When scientists take this stance, they may do so with a humility that acknowledges the limitations of their enterprise; or they may do it with a contempt for the politicians and other lesser breeds who will inevitably mess up anything so pure as science. In either case they tend to isolate science from the whole of human social existence.

Both these simplifications misconstrue the nature of ethical decision. I said earlier that scientific technology requires of men decisions that are not purely scientific but that involve values and conflicts of interest and are therefore ethical and political. The counterproposition is that in our technological world ethical and political decisions that are uninformed by science are likely to be naive and self-defeating. Particularly in the areas of public policy, all decisions have an informational component that is often utterly dependent on scientific inquiry, as well as an irreducibly ethical component that rests in man's commitments and his sense of the meaning of his existence.

If science does not itself provide ethical answers to the social perplexities of our time, no source that neglects science is likely to provide those answers. A religious ethic, for example, cannot use the traditions of the sacred scripture of the religious community as a source of ethical prescriptions for questions that were not traditionally raised in anything like their contemporary form. To take the examples I have been using—weaponry, population, genetics, and ecology—none of the traditional faiths contain codes of conduct for the twentieth century. Contemporary mankind must devise its own codes, which will be temporarily useful until revised to meet the next changes in the situation. And, even when ethics is most innovative, it is likely to find its perceptions sharpened, its compassion enlarged, and its awareness of the human condition deepened by insights of faith. The convictions that life is good, that our neighbor matters, that humanity owes some appreciation to nature, that contemporary man has an obligation to future man, that love exalts life, that man does not live by bread alone—all such convictions are supported only within the context of a faith that presupposes them.

Since scientific and ethical roles interact so intimately, there can be no neat division of labor between them. The scientist, I have said, does not determine the uses of his achievements. But as a human being, he cares. He may agonize. He may participate as a citizen in the political processes that have so much to do with his own opportunities, but he does not have the decisive voice in those processes. Scarcely any panel of scientists, if they had been given the power, would have assigned the priorities that have actually been given to exploration of the moon and development of a supersonic transport. These and other priorities were assigned by a social-political process that mobilizes and directs energies of higher education, industry, and the state. The assignment of priorities is a social decision, expressing the values and purposes or the commitments and faiths of a society as its power structures perceive them and act upon them.

Since World War II, scientists have become increasingly aware of both their own importance to government and the importance of governmental decisions to them. This double recognition, combined with the awesome realization of the portentous nature of their own accomplishments, has led to an increasing effort by some scientists to influence the process of ethical and political decision making. One of the earliest results was the publication of the *Bulletin of Atomic Scientists*. More recently there has been a change of mood in the professional societies of both the natural and social scientists, sometimes combined with dramatic confrontations between generational and ideological groups, as the traditional scientific detachment gives way to social involvement.

Yet the entry of scientists into the arena of public discussion has shown once again how intricate are the relations between scientific inquiry and ethical judgment. It turns out that both the advocates and the opponents of almost any cause can find scientific experts to testify on opposite sides. When the citizen who is not a scientist examines the argument, he may find that he feels utterly incompetent to judge between conflicting testimonies of experts whose detailed arguments he cannot understand. But he quickly comes to suspect that something besides technical expertise is expressed in the testimony. He may conclude that the argument is understandable less in terms of highly sophisticated scientific knowledge than in terms of the sociology of knowledge, as described by Karl Marx, Karl Mannheim, and their many successors.

This is only to say that the scientist, like everyone else, is a human being as well as a specialist. As a person he is influenced by his social situation. His interests and his commitments tell him that a program is or is not good, that it is or is not worth a major effort. And his conviction about the worth of the effort influences his judgment about its feasibility.

The controversy over the development of the ABM (anti-ballistic missile) gives a vivid illustration of the relationship between scientific expertise and ethical judgment. Scientists in the fields most intimately related to the program were sharply divided in their judgments on both the ethical-political and the technological issues at stake.

In 1969 Daniel D. McCracken, a widely recognized specialist on computers and the author of ten textbooks in the field, took the initiative in organizing Computer Professionals Against ABM. The Executive Committee and the sponsors included many of the most eminent computer specialists in the country, among whom were pioneers in both theoretical and practical aspects of computer science-technology. Altogether the support of some 500 specialists was enlisted, and they endorsed a statement that began as follows:

> We, the undersigned members of the computing profession, wish to record our professional judgment that there are grave doubts as to the technical feasibility of the computer portion of the Safeguard Antiballistic Missile system. These doubts range from a profound skepticism that the computing system could be made to work, to a conviction that it could not.[18]

The remainder of the statement gave the evidence and logic supporting the position.

It should be noted that the statement concerned a scientific-technological judgment. If scientists operated in a realm of pure objectivity according to a clearly defined scientific method, it would be conceivable that any argument over such a statement would depend exclusively on technical data and judgments, abstracted from such irrelevant matters as the employment of the researcher or the source of his funds and his political beliefs. It might then be expected that some militaristic hawks would concur in the statement and that some ardent doves would reject it, inasmuch as the statement concerned solely the technical feasibility of a computer system. Yet only an incredibly naive observer of the social process would expect such a consequence. Obviously the debate did not in fact shape up that way.

The Computer Professionals Against ABM were motivated by a social concern. Certainly the initiators of the movement believed the arms race to be harmful and the deployment of the ABM to be a misallocation of national resources. But, as a group of scientists-technologists, they claimed only the authority of their discipline and directed their argument to technical points. They sought to avoid any falsification of evidence or any fallacious argument. They wanted their statement to stand rigorous scientific scrutiny and to validate itself on its own grounds. Yet they were quite aware of the social motivations that prompted their activity.

---

[18]Daniel D. McCracken, *Ethical Problems of the Expert Witness in National Decision Making Involving the Assessment of Technology*, unpublished thesis in the library of Union Theological Seminary, 1970.

As it turned out—inevitably, I am tempted to say—the Pentagon had no difficulty in finding experts to testify that the computer system was feasible. It did not have to look hard for such experts, because it had them on the payroll. This issue became evident in the hearings of the Subcommittee on International Organization and Disarmament Affairs of the Senate Foreign Relations Committee in hearings in March, May, and July of 1969. Senator J. W. Fulbright pointed out that all the scientists testifying that the ABM was workable were currently or recently employees of the Pentagon or its contractors. Deputy Defense Secretary David Packard, after an embarrassing and less-than-candid effort to claim support from an "independent" expert, said:

> Senator Fulbright, I do not consider that when you are involved with scientific matters it is important whether you have people outside the Defense Department or not. Scientists, to me, are objective about such matters.[19]

The absurdity of the final sentence, in the context of extensive testimonies that pointed in the directly opposite direction, comes directly to the point of my concern. It is not simply that, as is commonly recognized, scientists are human beings, subject to varied human motives in their nonscientific roles. It is the even more significant fact that science always operates in a cultural context and that even highly technical scientific opinions are likely to be influenced by economic, political, ethical, and religious factors.

I do not intend to say this judgmentally, although it may have some judgmental significance. Certainly I do not condemn the scientist because his wisdom is not an angelic, extra-mundane wisdom. I am inclined to think the better of him if he is recognizably a human being, especially if he acknowledges the fact and takes some steps to guard against ideological distortions of his perceptions and reasoning.

From this situation I would move to two conclusions about the role of science and scientists in shaping public policy. First, some institutionalized effort should be made to draw on the judgment of panels of scientists who are a step removed from immediate participation in projects so that some scientific testimony is available from specialists not testifying directly for their own efforts and employers. (To that extent I still see some validity in the classical ideal of scientific objectivity.) Second, the rest of us in the body politic, although recognizing the immense importance of science in contributing to public policy, need not be intimidated into silence on public issues by the prestige of men with knowledge and skills that we lack. Particularly when such specialists are not unanimous, it may be that

[19]Ibid.

their opinions flow not solely from their expertise but also from their human prejudices and commitments; and in that area we have as much right to enter into policy making as they.

III. CHRISTIANITY AND THE EXPLOITATION OF NATURE

The ecological crisis requires a religious reformation. This is a judgment heard repeatedly from contemporary prophets and critics, often in the context of a severe criticism of the biblical and Christian tradition. No longer is the issue taken from the old battle of science and religion; today the common charge is not that religion opposes science but that it has endorsed too ardently a scientific technology that is destroying man's environment and threatening the human race.

The charges have logical force. If, as I have argued, the uses of science are determined by the purposes, values, and ethical sensitivities of society, and if these uses have become as threatening as many ecologists and demographers say, then any remedy must include some change in the commitments and ethical awareness of the society. And that means a reformation of established religion, whether in its most traditional or its most currently secular forms. This is precisely the judgment of Paul Goodman.

> To meet the historical crisis of science at present, for science and technology to become prudent, ecological, and decentralized requires . . . a kind of religious transformation. . . .Thus the closest analogy I can think of is the Protestant Reformation, a change of moral allegiance, liberation from the Whore of Babylon, return to the pure faith.[20]

Somewhat comparable to Goodman's argument is that of Charles A. Reich in *The Greening of America*. Even if (as I believe) he is utterly unconvincing in contending that questions of political and economic organization are, for the present at least, "insignificant, even irrelevant," he is persuasive in pointing to the importance of a change of "consciousness," which he specifically describes as a "conversion."[21]

In a study prepared for the National Council of Churches, economist Kenneth Boulding has described the ethical change required by the combined growth of population and technology with their resultant consumption of resources and pollution. In the past, he suggests, men could live

---

[20]"Can Technology Be Humane?" *New York Review of Books*, November 20, 1969, p. 33.

[21]New York: Random House, Inc., 1970. The citations are from p. 357 and pp. 223–24.

like cowboys on the illimitable plains; they appropriated infinite resources, had plenty of space to dump their wastes, and could always move on. Now, to use a metaphor that Boulding helped to make famous, they live on a spaceship.

> We have to visualize the earth as a small, rather crowded spaceship, destination unknown, in which man has to find a slender thread of a way of life in the midst of a continually repeatable cycle of material transformations. In a spaceship, there can be no inputs or outputs. The water must circulate through the kidneys and the algae, the food likewise, the air likewise. . . . In a spaceship there can be no sewers and no imports.
>
> Up to now the human population has been small enough so that we have not had to regard the earth as a spaceship. We have been able to regard the atmosphere and the oceans and even the soil as an inexhaustible reservoir, from which we can draw at will and which we can pollute at will. There is writing on the wall, however. . . . Even now we may be doing irreversible damage to this precious little spaceship.[22]

Boulding is not one of those who urge a moratorium on technological development in order that mankind may have a little time to adjust to its own swift changes. On the contrary, he thinks that technological progress must move speedily in order to meet the twin threats of exhaustion of resources and pollution.[23] But the technology must operate within the context of an ethic of parsimony rather than of exploitation. At this point Boulding, himself a Quaker Christian, makes some ambivalent judgments on the Christian tradition. He proposes that the ethic of the Sermon on the Mount will be more appropriate than ever in the past; it will no longer be a counsel of perfection but a necessity of survival for the fragile society of the spaceship, in which "we had better learn to love our enemies, or we will destroy each other."[24] On the other hand, he proposes that the Judeo-Christian tradition, "where God often is set off against nature," must learn from the traditions of Asian religion. "The East has never had any illusions about being able to conquer nature, and has always regarded man as living in a somewhat precarious position, as a guest of doubtful welcome, shall we say, in the great household of the natural world." Western aggressiveness toward nature may have been a prerequisite for the scientific revolution, but the time has come for "an ethic of conservation rather than of conquest."[25]

Shortly after Boulding's essay, historian Lynn White, Jr. developed

[22]Kenneth E. Boulding, *Human Values on the Spaceship Earth* (New York: National Council of Churches, 1966), p. 6.

[23]Kenneth E. Boulding, *The Meaning of the 20th Century* (New York: Harper and Row, Publishers, 1964).

[24]Boulding, *Human Values on the Spaceship Earth*, p. 13.

[25]Ibid., p. 14.

the same theme in an address at the Washington meeting of the American Association for the Advancement of Science in 1966. Later published in *Science* and reprinted in several settings, this address has become one of the landmarks of the contemporary ecological movement. Himself a churchman, White gives a stinging rebuke to the Christian tradition at exactly the point on which some of its representatives had been making their proudest boasts.[26]

Historians and theologians have long pointed out that technological progress may have more than an accidental relationship to biblical faith. Animistic, polytheistic, and pantheistic religions set up inhibitions against man's inquiry into, and domination of, nature, since they find the world to be inhabited with deities or to be itself divine. The radical monotheism of the Bible desacralizes nature and smashes the taboos that have so often thwarted man's investigations. The world is robbed of divinity; God has made it and has given man dominion over it. The appropriation of nature is henceforth not a transgression on God's prerogatives but an act of obedience. Thus Arend van Leeuwen saw the gift of Christianity as "liberation . . . from the fetters of 'sacred' tradition, together with the renewal of society in the direction of a truly secular and man-made order of life."[27] Soon thereafter Harvey Cox hailed both biblical faith and Barthian theology for dismissing myth and ontology with the consequence that "man's freedom to master and shape, to create and explore now reaches out to the ends of the earth and beyond."[28]

Without referring specifically to these writers, White rebuts them. He accepts their premise: "The victory of Christianity over paganism was the greatest psychic revolution in the history of our culture." And he sees the deposit of that victory persisting in contemporary life even when it has forgotten its Christian nurture. But instead of acclaiming the achievement, White points to its devastating consequences: "Especially in its Western form, Christianity is the most anthropocentric religion the world has seen. . . . By destroying pagan animism, Christianity made it possible to exploit nature in a mood of indifference to the feelings of natural objects."[29] For the ecological destructiveness of modern man, he maintains, "Christianity bears a huge burden of guilt."[30]

[26]Lynn White, Jr., "The Historical Roots of Our Ecologic Crisis," *Science*, 155 (March 10, 1967), 1203. Reprinted in Lynn White, Jr., *Machina ex Deo* (Cambridge, Mass.: MIT Press, 1969); also in The Environmental Handbook, ed. Garrett De Bell (New York: Ballantine Books, Inc., 1970).
[27]*Christianity in World History* (New York: Charles Scribner's Sons, 1965), pp. 419–20. (First Dutch edition, 1954.)
[28]Harvey Cox, *The Secular City* (New York: The Macmillan Company, 1965), p. 82.
[29]White, *Science*, 155, 1205.
[30]Ibid., p. 1206.

Because of the depth of this religious error, White thinks that technology cannot rescue us from its own effects.

> More science and more technology are not going to get us out of the present ecologic crisis until we find a new religion, or rethink our old one. . . . Both our present science and our present technology are so tinctured with orthodox Christian arrogance toward nature that no solution for our ecologic crisis can be expected from them alone. Since the roots of our trouble are so largely religious, the remedy must also be essentially religious, whether we call it that or not. We must rethink and refeel our nature and destiny.[31]

Like Boulding, White sees some possible help in the religions of the East, particularly Zen Buddhism. But, doubtful of its relevance to the West, he proposes a recovery of the insight of St. Francis of Assisi, who placed man in "a democracy of all God's creatures."

> With him the ant is no longer simply a homily for the lazy, flames a sign of the thrust of the soul toward union with God; now they are Brother Ant and Sister Fire, praising the Creator in their own ways as Brother Man does in his. . . . His unique view of nature and of man rested on a unique sort of pan-psychism of all things animate and inanimate, designed for the glorification of their transcendent Creator, who, in the ultimate gesture of cosmic humility, assumed flesh, lay helpless in a manger, and hung dying on a scaffold.[32]

I have quoted White at some length, both because of the forcefulness of his argument and because of its wide influence. An adequate appraisal of it would require attention to its historical detail, which I have not reproduced here. Yet I must ask two questions that may require qualification of White's thesis. First, has the relationship of Christianity to science-technology, whether an occasion for praise or for blame, been so direct and unequivocal as White maintains? Second is Franciscan Christianity so helpful as he suggests?

To start with the second question, St. Francis may have been more ambivalent toward nature than White acknowledges. To nominate St. Francis as "a patron saint for ecologists" is so daring and alluring an idea, in this age so far removed from his spirit, that I have no desire to search for flaws in Franciscan theology. Yet the asceticism of St. Francis, particularly with its deep distrust of sex and womanhood, raises perplexing issues about the adequacy of his theology of nature. Can Christians adequately appreciate nature while rejecting so fundamental an aspect of their own

[31]Ibid., pp. 1206, 1207.
[32]Ibid.

nature? Are there not strains in biblical thought that are more helpful on this issue?

To return to the first question, both the scientific revolution and the Christian tradition are exceedingly complex and rich in variety. White knows this, but he may not give it sufficient attention. He does not claim that Christianity was the sole cause of the Western scientific-technological movement; he maintains only that it was a necessary cause. But in concentrating his attention on it, he neglects other causes unrelated to Christianity. And he neglects the diversity of strains within the Christian tradition.[33]

Long before St. Francis there was one who said: "Consider the lilies of the field, how they grow; they neither toil nor spin; yet I tell you, even Solomon in all his glory was not arrayed like one of these" (Matt. 6:28–29). And even before Christ there is the tradition of Psalm 104 with its testimonies of God's concern for wild asses, storks, cattle, wild goats, lions, and the innumerable creatures of the sea. There is Noah, bidden to save the birds and beasts and reptiles no less than man. There is also Jonah, sent to Nineveh because of God's concern for the six score thousand people "and also much cattle," and there are the Messianic prophecies that promise a redemption to nature as truly as to man. And there is Job, gasping in amazement at the crocodile and hippopotamus, of no conceivable use to him—evidence that God did not create nature solely for man's use.

From the diverse themes in the Scripture have come a variety of theological traditions. Dostoevski's Alyosha Karamazov, embracing the Russian soil in ecstatic exultation and pondering the meaning of the grain of wheat as a symbol of death and resurrection, expresses one of these traditions. Martin Luther expresses another in his sacramentalism, insisting finite objects of nature are capable of communicating the infinite God. William Temple gives voice to still another theme, with his "Christian materialism" and his idea of the "sacramental universe," in which all nature and all the universe are the outward and visible sign of an inward and spiritual grace.[34]

Despite Temple's influence the main thrust of recent Protestantism has not followed the theme of his *Nature, Man and God,* with its union

[33]White takes no account of the prior refutation of his historical argument by Jacques Ellul (see Ellul's *Technological Society,* pp. 32–38). White and Ellul are so knowledgeable and cogent in their historical reasoning that a direct confrontation between them would do much to clarify the issue on which they disagree. See also L. Harold DeWolf, *Responsible Freedom* (New York: Harper & Row, Publishers, 1971), pp. 244–50.

[34]*Nature, Man and God* (London: Macmillan and Co., Ltd., 1949), especially Chap. 19.

of elements from Whitehead's metaphysics and from the moderately orthodox Anglican theological tradition. For the most part, theology in this epoch of world war and repeated political crisis has neglected the first term of Temple's title and has concentrated on man and God. Sometimes Karl Barth's reinterpreted Calvinism has been set against Temple's Anglican sacramentalism. But just here is an interesting issue. In many an account of modern culture, Calvinism and Puritanism have been assigned the villain's role, getting the blame for an obsolescent work ethic and a bourgeois insensitivity to nature and art. Yet we must ask how much a latter-day cultural Protestantism, appropriately described by Max Weber, has to do with theological Calvinism. Calvin himself maintained that God is "the Lord and Governor of nature, who uses all the elements according to his will for the promotion of his own glory." God can make of any object of nature a sacrament, as he did of the tree of life that he showed to Adam and Eve and of the rainbow that he showed to Noah. Calvin saw nothing unscientific in this sacramental awareness. He knew well that the rainbow is "a refraction of the rays of the sun on the opposite clouds" and that it has no "efficacy in restraining" flood waters. Still he recognized it as a sign communicating God's promises.[35]

It is perhaps ironical that Christian theology, long accused of sabotaging a healthy humanism by demeaning man before God, should suddenly be under assault for an exaggerated anthropocentrism. The logical conclusion may be that the Christian tradition encompasses many diverse strands and that all investigations of historical causation are likely to be misleadingly simple. The fact remains that modern man is suffering the consequences of a culture-religion (whether in Christian or secularized versions) that has neglected the importance of nature. Now the ecological crisis is showing that such a truncated religion is both inadequate and dangerous.

But there are theologies that recognize the significance of nature. Among these are some that make imaginative efforts to deal with the issues of religion and science, especially through the use of process philosophy, which takes nature seriously both as discerned by science and as recognized by man in himself. There are others that, without explicitly working on the detailed problems, make within their belief system a place for nature that encourages both appreciation and further inquiry. Among these I would put the "radical monotheism" of H. Richard Niebuhr. Written shortly before the ecological furor, it established a theological perspective helpful to the problems now so suddenly demanding attention.

[35]John Calvin, *Institutes of the Christian Religion*, IV, xiv, 18. I am grateful to Frederick Elder, who in his book *Crisis in Eden* (Nashville: Abingdon Press, 1970) has called this passage to my attention.

Niebuhr described a double movement characteristic of Christian theology. It is a dialectical movement of secularization and sanctification. Radical monotheism destroys all the idols that claim men's allegiance; in this sense it is iconoclastic and secularizes the world. Yet radical monotheism sanctifies all things as the creation of the one God. So Niebuhr could write as follows:

> Now every day is the day that the Lord has made; every nation is a holy people called by him into existence in its place and time and to his glory; every person is sacred, made in his image and likeness; every living thing, on earth, in the heavens, and in the waters is his creation and points in its existence toward him; the whole earth is filled with his glory; the infinity of space is his temple, where all creation is summoned to silence before him.[36]

Such a belief does not solve all problems, but it makes a place for all problems, and the latter is a wiser function of theology than the former. In particular this belief calls attention to the problem of suffering, which is inherent in the whole structure and process of nature; but suffering has always been a major concern of any faith that centers in the cross, and it cannot be evaded by theology.

To some it may seem inconsistent with the rigor of scientific method and the assumption of the autonomy of nature to bring to any scientific inquiry a prior assumption of faith that this world communicates a divine meaning. But to others it is fully as unreasonable to bring to inquiry an ascetic negation or skepticism about such meaning. I will let a scientist, Loren Eiseley, speak to that issue—without claiming that he supports any particular beliefs of my own.

> Man has a belief in seen and unseen nature. He is both pragmatist and mystic. . . . I shall want to look at this world from both the empirical point of view and from one which also takes into account that sense of awe and marvel which is part of man's primitive heritage, and without which man would not be man.[37]

No one has yet put together the comprehensive picture of the universe that adequately relates the two ways of apprehending experience. Perhaps no one ever will. But the effort, arduous and tentative, is worthwhile. And while it goes on, we may find help in the advice of Whitehead that when man has trouble weaving together different experiences that

[36]H. Richard Niebuhr, *Radical Monotheism and Western Culture* (New York: Harper & Row, Publishers, 1960), pp. 52–53.
[37]*The Firmament of Time* (New York: Atheneum Publishers, 1968), pp. 4, 8.

are in themselves convincing, he will be wiser to hang on to all the experiences than to suppress some for the sake of a prematurely unified scheme.[38]

> *ROGER L. SHINN is the Reinhold Niebuhr Professor of Social Ethics at Union Theological Seminary and Adjunct Professor of Religion at Columbia University. Among his many writings are* Life, Death and Destiny, Tangled World, *and most recently,* Man: The New Humanism. *Some of his essays and articles deal with ethical issues in population, genetics, and ecology. He was chairman of the Committee on Church and Economic Life of the National Council of Churches and is cochairman of the U.S.A. Task Force on the Future of Mankind and the Role of the Churches in a World of Science-Based Technology.*

[38]Alfred North Whitehead, *Science and the Modern World* (New York: The Macmillan Company, 1925), Chap. 9, "Religion and Science."

IAN G. BARBOUR

9

Attitudes Toward Nature and Technology

The American public is slowly becoming aware of the devastation of
the earth. We are poisoning our air and water with chemicals, fumes,
sewage, detergents, pesticides, radioactivity, noise, and heat. We dump 28
billion bottles and 48 billion cans each year. In a few decades we have
exterminated animal species that required hundreds of millions of years
to come into being. These facts are finally becoming widely known.

But the preceding chapters have suggested that ecological concern
will be short-lived and ineffectual unless it deals with the values and social
institutions that have led to this ravaging of the environment. The basic
disease is man's exploitative attitude toward both nature and his fellow
man. If we treat a succession of symptoms—seeking technical remedies
for one form of pollution after another—the task will be endless. Unless
the disease is cured, it will simply break out in new forms as men violate
the web of life in new ways. Fetid rivers and acrid air testify to our
failure to recognize our interdependence with the natural order. They
also testify to the failures of a social order in which technological policy is
determined more by private profit and national pride than by concern for
human welfare and the preservation of the earth.

In this concluding chapter, I will start by looking again at some
biblical views of nature and then suggest three aspects of an ecological
theology and an ecological ethic: man's unity with nature, God's

immanence in nature, and political responsibility for technology. Finally some ethical issues regarding the control of pollution and population and the redirection of technology are set forth. Hopefully this will bring together some of the themes of earlier chapters and carry them further into the realm of practical applications and social policies.[1]

I. BIBLICAL ATTITUDES
TOWARD NATURE

Attitudes toward nature in Western civilization have been influenced historically by the biblical doctrine of creation, which expressed the conviction that the world is orderly, dependable, and intelligible. Moreover if the realm of nature is created by God, it is essentially good rather than evil or illusory. In the Genesis narrative it is said of every created thing: "And God saw that it was good." Both Judaism and early Christianity endorsed affirmative attitudes toward nature. God is served *in* the world, not by renouncing it or by withdrawing to a separate religious sphere. These assumptions became part of the outlook of Western man and, according to most historians, contributed indirectly to the rise of modern science. If the universe is orderly and good, man is free to understand and use it.[2]

Biblical religion differed from most ancient religions in asserting that the world is neither divine nor demonic. This "desacralization" or "disenchantment" of nature has been noted by such recent theologians as Arend van Leeuwen and Harvey Cox, who are enthusiastic about technology and optimistic about man's power.[3] They point out that the Bible looks on nature as an essentially neutral sphere that man as a responsible historical agent is free to utilize. Western man was liberated from fear of the divine or the demonic in nature; the biblical world view brought with it an openness to historical change and a sense of responsibility for the future.

It should be noted that the religion of Israel arose amid surrounding religions that celebrated the vitalities of nature. Israel was convinced that she had come to know God first through crucial historical events, and only

---

[1] A brief version of several portions of this essay appeared as "An Ecological Ethic" in *Christian Century*, October 7, 1970.

[2] M. B. Foster, "The Christian Doctrine of Creation and the Rise of Modern Natural Science," *Mind*, 43 (1934), 466; 44 (1935), 439; 45 (1936), 1. The first of these along with several other interesting selections is reprinted in Daniel O'Connor and Francis Oakley, eds., *Creation: The Impact of an Idea* (New York: Charles Scribner's Sons, 1969).

[3] Arend van Leeuwen, *Christianity in World History*, tr. H. H. Hoskins (New York: Charles Scribner's Sons, 1965); Harvey Cox, *The Secular City* (New York: The Macmillan Company, 1965).

subsequently came to see the hand of God in the sphere of nature. She took the pagan nature festivals of the agricultural year and turned them into festivals commemorating formative events in her past, even though some of the earlier nature symbolism was retained in her liturgy. Professor Pelikan has suggested that perhaps Israel overreacted to the dangers of the nature-religions, with their tendency to deify natural vitalities. Today, he suggests, we must still start from history rather than nature, but we can go on to ascribe greater religious significance to the latter.[4]

In addition to these ideas of the orderliness, goodness, and desacralization of nature, there is in the creation story an apparent justification for man's power over it. Man is told to "be fruitful and multiply, and fill the earth and subdue it, and have dominion over the fish of the sea and over the birds of the air and over every living thing" (Gen. 1:28). Man is called to name the animals and to tend the garden. Psalm 8 says: "Thou hast given him dominion over the works of thy hands; thou hast put all things under his feet." Here is one of the historical roots of man's subjugation of his environment. Man is portrayed as separate from nature, rather than as an integral part of it. From such a passage one might almost conclude that the natural order has no reason for existence except for man's use. A one-sided emphasis on this theme of dominion seems to have contributed to Western man's exploitative outlook. In his influential article in *Science*, Lynn White states that "Christianity bears a huge burden of guilt" for environmental deterioration:

> Especially in its Western form, Christianity is the most anthropocentric religion the world has seen. Christianity, in absolute contrast to ancient paganism and Asia's religions (except perhaps Zoroastrianism), not only established a dualism of man and nature but also insisted that it is God's will that man exploit nature for his proper ends.... Hence we shall continue to have a worsening ecologic crisis until we reject the Christian axiom that nature has no reason for existence save to serve man.[5]

In the present crisis, as Huston Smith has pointed out, there is much that we could learn from Eastern religions about respect for nature. Chinese Taoism expresses a sense of man's harmony and unity with nature. Buddhism encourages reverence for all living creatures and appreciation for the beauty of the natural world. Contemplation rather than conquest

---

[4]Jaroslav Pelikan, "The Return to Nature," in D. E. Smucker, ed., *Rockefeller Chapel Sermons* (Chicago: University of Chicago Press, 1967).

[5]Lynn White, Jr., "The Historical Roots of Our Ecologic Crisis," *Science*, 155 (1967), 1203; reprinted in Paul Shepard and Daniel McKinley, eds., *The Subversive Science* (Boston: Houghton Mifflin Company, 1969), pp. 347, 350.

is advocated in the Hindu tradition. But it might be valuable in the American context to examine further the resources for new attitudes within our own culture. Moreover, if our religious tradition has had a share of the blame for our predicament, it has a special responsibility for encouraging new attitudes.

Some of the needed correctives can be found in the recovery of biblical themes that have been neglected:

1. *Man's responsibility for nature.* Man does not have absolute dominion, for he is responsible to God. "The earth is the Lord's" because he created it. The land belongs ultimately to God, and man is only a trustee or steward. He is vice-regent, responsible for the welfare of those entrusted to him. C. F. D. Moule holds that the statement that man is created "in the image of God" refers especially to the delegation of responsibility; only when distorted by human greed and pride does the concept of dominion become arrogance and ruthless exploitation. The theme of stewardship recurs frequently in the biblical record.[6]

2. *Nature's intrinsic value.* The created order is valued in itself, not simply as an instrument for man's purposes. God is said to delight in the earth and in the manifold variety of life, quite apart from man (Job 38–39; Ps. 104). Nature praises its creator (Pss. 19, 89, etc.). In the first chapter of Genesis, each form of life is pronounced good before man is on the scene. The Sabbath is a day of rest for the earth and living things as well as for man; and every seventh year, the sabbatical year, the fields are to lie fallow (Lev. 25:1). The land has its rights, and will cry out if misused.[7]

Many biblical passages express appreciation and wonder in response to nature. Recall how Job was finally overwhelmed by the majesty of natural phenomena. Jesus said that God notices the sparrow's fall. Value pervades all life, not just human life. Furthermore, nature participates in the drama of redemption and will share in the ultimate harmony, as portrayed in the symbolic vision of the end of days when "the wolf shall dwell with the lamb, and the leopard shall lie down with the kid" (Isa. 11:6). Paul imagines that "the whole creation has been groaning in travail to-

---

[6]See C. F. D. Moule, *Man and Nature in the New Testament* (Philadelphia: Fortress Press, 1967); Richard A. Baer, "Conservation: An Arena for the Church's Action," *Christian Century*, January 8, 1969, p. 40; Lee Umphrey, "Pitfalls and Promises of Biblical Texts as a Basis for a Theology of Nature," in Glenn C. Stone, ed., *A New Ethic for a New Earth* (New York: Friendship Press, 1971).

[7]Bernhard W. Anderson, *Creation versus Chaos* (New York: Association Press, 1967); Edmund Jacob, *Theology of the Old Testament*, tr. A. Heathcote and P. Allcock (New York: Harper & Row, Publishers, 1958).

gether until now, but it will all take part in the final fulfillment (Rom. 8:19ff).

But there was incipient in Paul, and more strongly developed in the early centuries of Christian thought, a more negative appraisal. The gnostic estimation of the world as evil influenced the growth of an asceticism and life-denial that contrasts with the biblical affirmation of life. With the mood of despair attending the breakdown of Roman civilization, hope was increasingly transferred from this world to the next. With moral and social decline, the church saw itself as a sanctuary of moral purity separated from the corruption of the world. The dualism of body and soul, or more generally of matter and spirit, led to a devaluation of nature and sometimes outright hostility toward it. To Augustine the sphere of nature is fallen and corrupted, and the body is the main vehicle of human sin. The world was viewed, if not as a prison to be escaped, at least as a testing ground for human souls destined for another world. The life of animals was taken more as a parable for man than as a phenomenon of intrinsic value and interest; farfetched animal fables based on popular folklore were read as symbols of human virtues and vices. Man's superiority over nature was here expressed not by exploiting it but by dismissing it as irrelevant to eternal salvation.[8]

There were, of course, many strands in the complex thought of the early centuries when Greek and biblical thought interacted. The Greek fathers took a more positive view; to them the Logos was both the rational principle of the universe and the divine Word in Christ. In the thirteenth century, Thomas Aquinas attempted a synthesis of Aristotelian science and philosophy with biblical theology. Though reason and revelation remained separate sources of truth, he was convinced that if nature and grace both proceed from God, the two spheres are in harmony with each other. St. Francis of Assisi represents still another kind of response, a deep love of the natural world, a joy and sense of union with it. He saw nature as a living whole and all creatures as objects of God's love and hence as significant in their own right. St. Francis greeted the birds as brothers, extending the family relationship and the circle of God's love to include all created beings sharing a common dignity and equality under God. The Benedictine monasteries, on the other hand, combined respect for nature with practical wisdom and hard work; their monks brought productive agriculture and sound land management to many parts of Europe.

Most of the key figures in the rise of science in the seventeenth century expressed respect and admiration for the beauty and order of the

[8]Charles E. Raven, *Natural Religion and Christian Theology* (Cambridge: Cambridge University Press, 1953), Vol. 1.

universe. Kepler believed that in understanding the motion of the planets he was thinking God's thoughts after him; Newton and Boyle held that nature displayed God's power and wisdom.[9] But with the growth of technology—whose goal is to control nature rather than to understand it—more exploitative and utilitarian motives predominated. The economic interests of the rising middle class, the competitiveness and rugged individualism of the capitalist ethos, the goals of economic productivity and efficiency—aided, no doubt, by the "Protestant ethic" of frugality, hard work, and dominion over the earth—all these encouraged a ruthlessness and arrogance toward nature unknown in earlier centuries. In the industrial revolution, the realm of nature was treated exclusively as a resource for man's use and a means for commercial profit. Additional factors contributed to exploitative attitudes on the American scene: a land of seemingly unlimited natural resources, a belief in a manifest destiny to subdue a continent and build a nation, a frontier that allowed for continued expansion into new territory, an industrial development that promised ever higher living standards. I will return in a later section to these distinctive problems of modern technology.

We cannot, then, expect to find any simple biblical theology of nature relevant for today. There are, in the Bible itself and in subsequent Christian thought, a diversity of views articulated in a succession of historical contexts—from early nature-religions, the disintegrating Roman empire, and the medieval church, down to the rise of modern science and finally industrial technology. The Bible can serve, rather, as a source of insights that must be explored in the light of new knowledge in our contemporary situation. Widespread pollution and overpopulation are novel problems that have never occurred before in history, and we cannot expect to find direct advice about them in Scripture. The growth of technology gives unprecedented power to control nature, for better or worse. Man confronts new crises and new options that have never existed previously.

We can, however, recover from the Bible the affirmative attitude toward the world that was sometimes lost amid later currents of other-worldliness and life-denial. We can recover its convictions that nature has intrinsic value and that man's dominion must be exercised responsibly. Above all we can find in biblical religion a far-reaching concern for man's welfare, a dedication to the neighbor's needs, which we now know are closely tied to the natural environment. We can reappropriate many of the basic biblical assumptions about nature, man, and God, but we must articulate them in new ways. Our approach, I submit, must be interdisciplinary.

[9]Richard S. Westfall, *Science and Religion in Seventeenth-Century England* (New Haven: Yale University Press, 1958).

The following sections examine three components of such an interdisciplinary theology of ecology: the unity of man and nature, the immanence of God, and the responsible control of technology.

II. MAN'S UNITY WITH NATURE

The Christian tradition has too often set man apart from nature. But today many fields of science, from ecology to molecular biology and evolutionary studies, provide evidence that man is part of the natural order and dependent on the intricate web of life. Ecology gives us a new understanding of man-in-environment. We are, for example, quite literally dependent on plants that take in carbon dioxide and give out the oxygen we breathe. When we pollute a lake, we destroy its water-purifying bacteria irreversibly and end by harming ourselves. John Donne's words can be extended to embrace the whole natural world: "No man is an Iland, intire of it selfe; every man is a peece of the Continent, a part of the maine."

Ecology is the study of the relations of organisms and their environments; it considers systems rather than isolated entities. It deals with communities of beings and the interconnectedness of living things. We live in subtly balanced networks, and the effects of our actions reverberate throughout the ecosystem. In a classic example, DDT used in Borneo for mosquito control was absorbed by flies, which were the chief food of a small lizard, the gecko; cats, which eat geckos, were affected; rats then thrived—and created sufficient threat of plague that additional cats had to be parachuted into the villages to control the rats.[10] In general, pesticides are long-lasting, and their effects are cumulative and sometimes irreversible. American women have in their breast milk concentrations of DDT three to ten times higher than the government allows in dairy milk for human consumption.

Ecology underscores three features of natural life: (1) *Interdependence*. Recall the complex cycles of elements and compounds (the nitrogen cycle or the water cycle, for example), the marvelous reciprocities and mutualities among organisms, the long food chains linking diverse species, the ways in which environments and life-support systems are themselves the product of living things. (2) *Diversity*. Homogeneous systems (such as one-crop agriculture or one-industry towns) are easily disrupted, whereas heterogeneous ones have greater capacity for change and adaptation. (3) *Vulnerability*. Delicate balances are easily upset, and the changes may be irreversible. Awareness of the dangers of intervention and

---

[10]Gordon Harrison, *Natural History*, 77 (1968), 9.

of the limits of adaptability does not, however, imply resistance to all change. It is sometimes assumed that "ecosystem" is a static concept representing a status quo that must never be tampered with. But even without man, natural systems are dynamic and constantly changing. The lesson of ecology is not the avoidance of change but recognition that changes introduced by man have far-reaching consequences.[11]

It might be mentioned parenthetically that one of the few positive aspects of some psychedelic experiences is a vivid awareness of the interdependence of self and environment, a capacity to feel one's identity as inseparable from surrounding processes. It has been claimed that psychedelic drugs encourage people to overcome their alienation from nature, to be conscious of themselves as focal points of networks of relations, and participants in wider fields. Perhaps man's intuitive experience of the interconnectedness of all things tends to be suppressed in our rationalistic and competitive culture with its myth of the self-sufficient individual.[12]

Consider next the evidence for man's unity with nature provided by molecular biology and evolution. The same four bases make up the DNA of almost all living things, and many of the proteins in different species are remarkably alike. The cytochrome enzyme in man is a string of 104 amino acids, of which 92 are identical in the horse and 82 in fish. Our genetic line goes back unbroken to the earliest organisms. We are, as it were, the thousandth cousin of an amoeba. We are kin to all creatures, sharing a common history, participating in a long creative process. We are part of the interwoven fabric of life that has taken 5 billion years to come into being.[13]

The early Darwinists, anxious to prove that man was a product of evolution, stressed similarities between human and animal life. They claimed that there were no essential differences between man and the higher apes. Today biologists recognize these affinities but are impressed also by man's unique capacities. Human language is now understood to be radically different from all communication among animals; man can use abstract symbols and general concepts to refer to what is not present. His power to remember the past and anticipate the future liberates him from his immediate time and place. He can respond to ideal possibilities

[11]See Shepard and McKinley, *The Subversive Science*; John Storer, *Man in the Web of Life* (New York: The New American Library, Inc., Mentor Books, 1968); Barry Commoner, *Science and Survival* (New York: The Viking Press, Inc., 1967); Edward Kormondy, *Concepts of Ecology* (Englewood Cliffs, N.J.: Prentice-Hall, Inc., 1969).

[12]Richard A. Underwood, "Ecological and Psychedelic Approaches to Theology," *Soundings*, 52 (1969), 365; Alan W. Watts, "The Individual as Man/World," in Shepard and McKinley, *The Subversive Science*.

[13]This theme is developed in Ian G. Barbour, *Science and Secularity: The Ethics of Technology* (New York: Harper & Row, Publishers, 1970), Chap. 4.

—to a vision of what ought to be as well as what is. In imagination and in act he can create the genuinely new. Man alone can deliberately plan the future—including his own further evolutionary development.

The distinctiveness of human culture has also been noted by many contemporary biologists. Cultural change is a new form of evolution very different from genetic change. The legacy of the past is transmitted to the future by education, the written word, and social institutions as well as by genes. Human culture is not something external to us, but is formulative of our psycho-social existence. Man is inherently a social being, for the individual self is constituted by its relationships. Furthermore, only man is self-conscious; he alone asks who he is and knows that he will die. His freedom to distinguish alternatives and to choose among them is the basis of his sense of moral responsibility. Man as personal agent can respond in love to the needs of his neighbor.

Man, in sum, is intimately related to other living forms—both within the present web of life and in the slow progression of an evolutionary development exhibiting historical continuity without sharp breaks—yet man is also unique in nature. Frederick Elder's typology in *Crisis in Eden* thus seems to me an oversimplification. He sets the "inclusionists," who include man in nature, against the "exclusionists," who stress the uniqueness of man. Because this sharp dichotomy allows no middle ground, Elder is forced to classify Teilhard de Chardin with the "exclusionists," neglecting Teilhard's strong convictions concerning the unity and continuity of the cosmic process.[14]

A contemporary doctrine of man, in my opinion, must express his unity with nature and his similarity to other forms of life without ignoring the distinctiveness of human existence. I believe that this requires the rejection of the body-soul dualism of classical Christian thought and a return to the biblical view of man as a unitary being. In the Bible, the self is conceived not as a separate entity but as a unified activity of thinking, feeling, and acting. Man is a personal agent, a responsible self interacting with other selves. Man is a social being whose relatedness is his very being. Biblical man is constituted by his relationships; he is who he is precisely as father, husband, citizen, and member of a covenanted people. The dominant image of person-in-community emphasizes this social dimension of selfhood.

Later Christian thought, under the influence of Greek dualism, sometimes imagined a disembodied soul imprisoned in an evil body. But the Bible itself looks on mind, body, and spirit as aspects of a personal unity. Oscar Cullmann insists that "the Jewish and Christian interpretation of

[14]Frederick Elder, *Crisis in Eden* (Nashville: Abingdon Press, 1970).

creation excludes the whole Greek dualism of body and soul."[15] In particular, the body is not the source of evil or something to be disowned, escaped, or denied. There is instead a positive acceptance of the body; man is an integral being, an active bodily self—a psychosomatic unity, as we would now phrase it.

Today we can look on man both as a biological organism and as a responsible self. He is a many-leveled unity, and the levels are not mutually exclusive. Some of these levels of organization and activity he shares with all matter, some he shares with all living things, some with all animal life, whereas some seem to be unique to man. Distinctive categories can be used to describe distinctive events occurring at higher levels, without denying their dependence on lower levels. Moreover, alternative models representing different modes of analysis of any system can be used. As linguistic philosophers remind us, there is a plurality of kinds of language that serve diverse functions; we can use several models of man that are valuable for different purposes. Man, in short, can be viewed both as biological organism and as responsible self within the community of life.[16]

The biblical recognition of human finitude and of anxiety in the face of death provides an additional insight into the motives that have resulted in ecological destruction. Man is tempted to seek a false security by amassing material goods. In his quest for power he uses other creatures as means to his own ambitions. Throughout human history, land and natural resources have been instruments of personal power and pride. This understanding of man will lead us to be realistic about entrenched structures of institutional power, which are not going to yield to romantic pleas for the preservation of wildlife or to altruistic appeals for the general welfare. Moreover, the Gospel's message of liberation from anxiety and of reconciliation overcoming estrangement can be seen to have repercussions not only in personal life and human relationships but in the way we treat our environment. Only the person released from anxiety and self-centeredness is free to love man and nature.

These distinctive features of human existence can be acknowledged without denying man's fundamental unity with nature. The first component of an ecological theology and an ecological ethic, then, is a new vision of our interdependence with the whole created order. We are part of a larger whole, a kingdom of life. We must recover a basic respect for all living things and a new awareness of our mutual participation in the community of life.

[15] Oscar Cullmann, *Immortality of the Soul or Resurrection of the Dead?* (New York: The Macmillan Company, 1958), p. 30.
[16] See Barbour, *Science and Secularity*, Chaps. 1 and 4.

III. GOD'S IMMANENCE IN NATURE

The second component of an ecological theology is a new formulation of the idea of divine immanence. The neglect of nature in orthodox
Christianity continued in the main theological movements of the first half
of the twentieth century. In neo-orthodoxy, nature remained the setting
for man's redemption. In existentialism, it was the impersonal stage for the
drama of personal existence. A radical separation between the realm of
history and the realm of nature has been typical of Protestant thought
since Kant. But today there is evidence of renewed interest in the religious
significance of the natural order. Joseph Sittler's address to the assembly
of the World Council of Churches in 1961 was a powerful plea for "the
care of the earth," a declaration that "nature as well as history is the
theatre of grace."[17] Especially in the process theology of Alfred North
Whitehead, Teilhard de Chardin, and their followers, a new understanding
of God's relation to the world has been articulated.

To start with, process thought elaborates a new view of nature itself.
In the Newtonian view, which prevailed until the last century, nature was
essentially static; all things were believed to have been created in their
present forms. The order of nature was held to be simple, reducible to a
few types of entity governed by a few basic laws. It was thought to be
determined, its future in principle predictable from knowledge of the
present. But today nature appears not as a machine but as a dynamic
process of becoming, always changing and developing, radically temporal
in character—an incomplete cosmos still coming into being. It is not simple
but highly complex and many-leveled, populated by many diverse types
of entities, describable by many diverse types of laws. Furthermore, it
seems to be in principle unpredictable, especially at the level of quantum
physics. Many scientific laws are statistical and do not allow prediction of
individual events. Gene recombinations and mutations are unrepeatable
occurrences producing unique individuals; particular sequences of con-
tingent historical circumstances and environmental changes have produced unique evolutionary species.

Process thinkers thus represent nature as a dynamic and creative
process, unified but diverse. They have stressed the organic interdependence of all creatures and their intrinsic value and have defended man's
continuity with the rest of nature. For them, mind and matter are not two
opposing principles or substances, but two patterns of events in systems

---

[17]Joseph Sittler, "Called to Unity," *Ecumenical Review*, 14 (January, 1962);
also his "A Theology of Earth," *The Christian Scholar*, 37 (1954), 367.

having many levels of organization. The world is a vast experiment, its future still undecided and open to new possibilities. Nature is a single creative drama in which both God and finite creatures participate.[18]

Process thought defends the idea of continuing creation rather than an initial divine act "at the beginning." Creativity continues as new forms of life come into being and as higher levels of consciousness and individuation appear. Both Whitehead and Teilhard avoid postulating a God who intervenes from outside at specific points and instead portray God's creativity immanent throughout the cosmic process. Man must now collaborate with God in bringing the world to completion. Teilhard writes: "Creation has never ceased. Its act is a great continuous movement spread out over the totality of time. It is still going on."[19] He speaks of grace at work throughout the cosmic process; if God is present in all things, the whole world has a sacramental character. Here is a life affirmation and a love of the earth reminiscent of St. Francis, an assertion of the value of this world as against any life-denying renunciation. In Teilhard, a mysticism of personal experience combines with an evolutionary monism to support an emphasis on God's immanence.[20]

In Whitehead, on the other hand, divine immanence in nature is represented through a detailed metaphysics in which God, past causes, and individual self-realization contribute jointly to the unfolding of every event.[21] Each entity must respond for itself, and nothing that happens is God's act alone. God does not act directly but rather influences the creatures to act, and their responses are genuinely their own. If I respond to God, the response is mine alone, not the product of irresistible grace; in the last analysis I must decide for myself. If there is genuine freedom and novelty in the world, then even God cannot know the future until the decisions have been made by individual agents. There are alternatives open until choices are made at a variety of centers of responsibility. God respects the freedom of his creatures. He is always one factor among many; he always acts with and through other causes. Here is a personal model of divine power as love, persuasion, and the evocation of response rather than as omnipotent coercion or predetermination. A number of theologians

---

[18]See Charles Birch, *Nature and God* (London: SCM Press, 1965); Richard H. Overman, *Evolution and the Christian Doctrine of Creation* (Philadelphia: The Westminster Press, 1967).

[19]Pierre Teilhard de Chardin, *Ecrits du temps de la guerre* (Paris: Editions Bernard Grasset, 1965), p. 149.

[20]See especially his *The Divine Milieu* (New York: Harper & Row, Publishers, 1960).

[21]Ivor Leclerc, *Whitehead's Metaphysics* (New York: The Macmillan Company, 1958); Daniel Williams, "How Does God Act? An Essay in Whitehead's Metaphysics," in W. L. Reese and E. Freeman, eds., *Process and Divinity* (LaSalle, Ill.: Open Court Publishing Co., 1964).

have carried further this Whiteheadian understanding of God's immanence in nature.[22]

Several recent writers have given attention to other dimensions of divine immanence. Frederick Elder sees religious significance in the threatening aspects of the natural order as well as in its beauty and creativity. He reminds us that there is a power of judgment as well as a power of grace at work in the world. When the unity of the universe is violated, the violators are punished. Man cannot with impunity ignore the welfare of the community of life. In nature as in history there is a moral order and an immanent judgment, of which "the wrath of God" was perhaps an overly anthropomorphic symbol. In judgment and in grace God operates not apart from natural forces but in and through them.[23]

Loren Eiseley's writings frequently convey a sense of awe, reverence, and wonder as he confronts the mystery and beauty of living creatures linked together across the immensities of time and space. He is a scientist of great sensitivity who expresses with poetic force the experience of the numinous. "For many of us," he writes, "the Biblical bush still burns and there is a deep mystery in the heart of a simple seed." Nature may be "one mask of many worn by the Great Face beyond." Standing in the desert as a flight of birds passes overhead, he reflects on their kinship with the creatures whose fossil bones he holds, creatures who looked on the world 50 million years ago. He contemplates the marvel of life and the greater marvel of man:

> If the day comes when the slime of the laboratory crawls under man's direction, we shall have great need of humbleness. It will be difficult for us to believe, in our pride of achievement, that the secret of life has slipped through our fingers and eludes us still. We will list all the chemicals and the reactions. The men who have become gods will pose austerely before the popping flashbulbs of news photographers, and there will be few to consider—so deep is the mind-set of an age—whether the desire to link life to matter may not have blinded us to the most remarkable characteristics of both.[24]

The writings of Eiseley and others engender a basic respect for the value of all living things, a sense of wonder and reverence for life. Such

[22]John B. Cobb, *A Christian Natural Theology* (Philadelphia: The Westminster Press, 1965); Charles Hartshorne, *Reality as Social Process* (New York: The Free Press, 1953); Peter Hamilton, *The Living God and the Modern World* (Philadelphia: United Church Press, Pilgrim Press, 1967).

[23]Elder, *Crisis in Eden*, p. 102.

[24]Loren Eiseley, *The Immense Journey* (New York: Random House, Inc., 1957), p. 208.

direct responses could influence men's actions more strongly than any abstract theory of divine immanence. We can come to feel, as well as to think, that the despoiling of the earth and the extermination of species are a sacrilege, a desecration of something precious. Brutality toward other forms of life is a violation of the sanctity and harmony of the larger order in which man's life is set. We can find new ways to celebrate the richness and diversity of life and our participation in it. One of the dangers in the technological mentality, as I will indicate below, is the impoverishment of experience and the objectification of nature.

IV. TECHNOLOGY AND POLITICAL RESPONSIBILITY

Let us turn now to look at technology, which is the most powerful instrument of man's dominion as well as the prime source of environmental deterioration. Moreover technology is directly related to human welfare and to the social context in which men live. The exploitation of nature and the exploitation of other human beings are inseparable; they reflect a common set of cultural values and a common framework of economic and political institutions. Pollution and urban blight are linked together as products of a technological society that is thing-oriented rather than person-oriented and life-oriented.

Furthermore, as a motive for an ecological ethic, concern for fellow man is as important as respect for nature. Without reverting to an exclusively man-centered viewpoint, I would assert that persons are indeed more valuable than other forms of life. If we should be sensitive to the suffering of animals, how much more should the suffering of people trapped in decaying ghettos be of concern to us. The prophetic ideal of social justice and human fulfillment puts new demands on us today. We now know that the neighbor in need is totally dependent on his environment and on the social institutions that surround him. Ours must be a political theology that leads to responsible action.

Despite the significant legislation that it has produced, the conservation movement has been limited in its long-run effects because it has tended to think of nature and man apart from this social context. Its victories are at best stopgaps in the face of the population explosion and burgeoning technological pollution. The movement has often been supported by relatively privileged groups, people who could afford hunting and fishing or vacations in National Parks. Conservationists have usually assumed that no fundamental changes in our society are needed. Like John Muir in the last century, they have often scorned the city and instead have urged escape from society and its problems into the beauty of the wilderness; as Paul Santmire points out, they have seldom been involved in the struggle for social justice.[25]

If we examine the impact of technology on human attitudes, then, we must grant that it has liberated people from backbreaking labor and has greatly improved standards of health. But it also seems to have encouraged the frantic pursuit of comfort. Ours is an acquisitive society that awakens false desires by deliberately fostering new cravings. A barrage of advertising stimulates our appetites as consumers and engenders an insatiable drive toward greater and greater affluence; it promotes wasteful consumption, planned obsolescence, and the production of luxury goods while basic needs around the world remain unmet. One American uses up resources faster than 50 citizens of India. It would be simply impossible for the whole world to consume energy and materials at the United States rate.

Another result of the technological mentality is the impoverishment of experience, the loss of man's imaginative and emotional life and the sensibilities expressed in poetry and art. A recent sociological study listed the following as among the main American value-orientations: achievement, active mastery, efficiency, progress, and success.[26] And these value-orientations are characteristic of our male-dominated society, which values the aggressive "masculine" qualities more than the nurturing, conserving, sensitive qualities associated with women—qualities which might contribute distinctively to an ecological conscience. Technological man is alienated from nature, treating it as an object to be used and manipulated. The calculating attitude of control and mastery militates also against the openness and receptivity that interpersonal relationships require. The I-Thou relation, as Buber calls it, requires availability, responsiveness, mutuality, and personal involvement, in contrast to the I-It pattern of manipulation and objective detachment. The danger here is that technological attitudes, which are necessary and valuable in their own domain, will so dominate life that important areas of human experience are jeopardized.

In this situation, biblical religion can witness to dimensions of human experience that are not accessible to technical reason. It can uphold the dignity and value of the person against all attempts to manipulate or control him. It can present a model of man as responsible self within a community of life, rather than as consumer or technician. It can cultivate and intensify human experience, richness of imagination, and

---

[25]H. Paul Santmire, "Ecology and Schizophrenia: Historical Dimensions of the American Crisis," *Dialog*, 9 (1970), 175, and his *Brother Earth* (New York: Thomas Nelson, Inc., 1970).

[26]Robin M. Williams, *American Society*, 2nd ed. (New York: Alfred A. Knopf, Inc., 1967), Chap. 11.

awareness of the sacred. It can provide a perspective for criticism of cultural values and reflection on the ends of human existence, a vision of a society in which technological progress is subordinate to man's true well-being. What is required here is a basic shift in values from a thing-oriented culture to one which is person-oriented and, beyond that, life-oriented. The biblical message can encourage sensitivity to the effects of unbridled technology on people and on nature, and awareness of the dangers when productive efficiency becomes our main goal. We are called to a more authentic human existence, not to greater affluence.

I submit, finally, that both pollution and poverty are products of our failure to devise adequate social controls over technology. Concern for ecology need not compete with concern for social justice; they converge in demanding a fundamental redirection of technology. Let me spell this out:

1. The dispossessed have benefited least from technology. Unemployment from automation hits the unskilled hardest. For example, a freeway is seldom used by the ghetto residents whose houses are torn down to make room for it. Government subsidy of supersonic planes would mainly benefit the skilled workers in aerospace industries and the affluent who can afford to fly. Black Americans are special victims of pollution, since they usually cannot escape the dirt, smog, and noise of the ghetto. Both within our nation and between nations, uncontrolled technology tends to increase the gap between the rich and the poor, and to reinforce existing power structures. (For instance, powerful lobbies from the auto and highway industries, and from insurance, oil and gas companies have worked to block public urban transit schemes.[27])

2. The "invisible hand" of the marketplace is inadequate to control technology. Classical laissez-faire economics assumed that if each person sought his own profits, the laws of supply and demand would regulate production and yield the social good. In the past, resources were bountiful, the detrimental social effects were tolerable, and private enterprise in the United States did engender productivity and higher standards of living—though not without great inequalities in the distribution of its benefits. Technology in particular became a major instrument of profit and power. The financial rewards often went to the person who could find new ways to exploit natural resources quickly and cheaply. Today the social cost of that exploitation is intolerably high, and new forms of taxes and regulations are needed so that the person who jeopardizes the general welfare is not rewarded. The influence of technological decisions is now so per-

[27]See Victor Ferkiss, *Technological Man* (New York: George Braziller, Inc., 1969).

vasive that it cannot be left to the vagaries of the marketplace. We breathe or suffocate together.

3. *The right of private property is not absolute.* We have assumed that land and natural resources are one's own to do with as one pleases. Entire landscapes have been destroyed by strip mining; redwood forests have been leveled for lumber. The westward sweep of settlement has been called "the greatest waste and destruction of natural resources in the shortest time in all history.[28] Half the productive top soil of our nation has been lost. Often the government has encouraged this rapid exhaustion of resources (e.g., by the oil depletion allowance). Today our legal structures are just beginning to recognize that the planet and its resources, on which we all depend, belong to everyone—and also to future generations. There is also increasing realization that water and air, which belong to us all, are a "commons" which in the public interest must be protected from the dumping of privately generated wastes.[29]

4. *The social costs of technological innovations must be paid for by their users.* Insofar as possible the price of an item should reflect its total social cost and not simply the immediate cost of production. The cost of resource conservation, pollution control, and waste disposal should be carried by the producer and hence ultimately by the consumer. If soft-drink manufacturers were assessed for the disposal of empty cans, they would try to minimize the total cost (production and disposal) and not just the cost of production. New methods of "social accounting" have been developed that allow at least some estimate of such costs. Uniform national standards for industrial effluents can be developed and enforced. Only in rare cases will special tax incentives for exceptionally expensive pollution-abatement equipment be needed.

Court action and new legislation are effective in curbing many forms of technological pollution. The beginning of environmental law is occurring through the extension of earlier concepts of "nuisance" and "trespass." But the contest between a citizens' group and a giant corporation or government agency is an unequal one, and the traditional legal structure has focused primarily on property rights and direct personal injuries. But there have been successful "class actions" in which an individual has sued not just as the injured party but on behalf of a wider group of citizens. In the "Scenic Hudson" case, a court of appeals prevented the construction of a power plant that would have marred an exceptionally beautiful stretch of the river. A constitutional amendment guaranteeing explicit

---

[28]Paul Knight, "The Politics of Conservation" in *Christians and the Good Earth* (Alexandria, Va.: The Faith-Man-Nature Group, 1967).

[29]Garrett Hardin, "The Tragedy of the Commons," *Science*, 162 (1968), 1243.

"environmental rights" would facilitate the formation of new laws (such as the prohibition of lead in gasoline).[30]

An important study of the processes by which decisions concerning technology are made has been prepared by a panel of the National Academy of Sciences. This report points out that economic profit and technical efficiency have been the main considerations in the development of new technologies; wider consequences for society have seldom been taken into account. No one is responsible for gathering in advance evidence of possible harmful effects or indirect social costs. By the time that deleterious repercussions are widespread, new industries and powerful vested interests (e.g., in a particular type of pesticide or detergent) are already strongly entrenched. The people most affected usually have no voice in the early stages of decision making:

> Indeed the very essence of the panel's concern about the narrowness of the criteria that currently dominate technological choices is the conviction that *the present system fails to give all affected interests effective representation in the crucial processes of decision. . . .* Present mechanisms frequently reflect the views, interests, enthusiasms, and biases of unduly narrow constituencies and create insufficient opportunities for meaningful participation in choices having major public consequences.[31]

According to this panel, decisions "should remain open to the widest range of responsible influence by all potentially interested groups and by surrogate representatives of interests too diffuse or too weak to generate effective spokesmen of their own."[32] The report proposes that offices devoted to the assessment of the social effects of technological development be established within several existing federal agencies. These offices would have the power to study and recommend but not to act, yet they would be close to the centers of power, namely the President and Congress. The report makes specific recommendations for: (1) A Technology Assessment Division within the existing Office of Science and Technology, which advises the President; (2) A Technology Assessment Division within the existing National Science Foundation, which would sign contracts with universities and government agencies and make grants to individual scholars for research on the social effects of new technologies; (3) A

[30]David Sive, "From Conservation to Environmental Law," *Motive*, April 1970, p. 90; Paul and Anna Ehrlich, *Population, Resources, Environment* (San Francisco: W. H. Freeman and Co., Publishers, 1970), Chap. 11.

[31]*Technology: Processes of Assessment and Choice*, Report of The National Academy of Sciences (Committee on Science and Astronautics, U.S. House of Representatives, 1969), pp. 41, 115.

[32]Ibid., p. 90; see also Harvey Brooks and Raymond Bowers, "The Assessment of Technology," *Scientific American*, 222 (February, 1970), p. 13.

Technology Assessment Service (paralleling the Legislative Reference Service)—or alternatively, a Joint Congressional Committee—to advise Congress and its various committees. I will suggest below that perhaps new federal departments with greater power of action are needed.[33]

National planning and control should go beyond the prevention of harmful consequences and should foster the positive development of technology in socially desirable directions. Technology is the greatest single influence on the future, and it is indeed subject to social control; it appears as an inevitable and autonomous force only because adequate mechanisms for its guidance have not been created. We have never had a coherent national policy for applied science. Instead we have had a mixture of laissez faire and crash programs in response to a succession of crises from Sputnik to pollution.

V. POLLUTION AND POPULATION

I cannot close without mentioning population control. There have been dozens of speeches and bills in Congress on pollution for every one on population. But measures against either pollution or poverty will be ineffective unless the population explosion is halted. Each day 324,000 babies are born on our globe, but only 133,000 persons die; so there are 190,000 more persons to feed every twenty-four hours. Each week the equivalent of the city of Cleveland is added to the world's population. Each year the increase is more than the entire population of France, Belgium, and Holland.

The rate of population increase is of course highest in the underdeveloped countries, which can least afford it. In Costa Rica or the Philippines the population doubles in 20 years; in Egypt or Kenya, the doubling time is 23 years. In order to keep even their present meager living standards, such countries would have to double their food production and double the number of doctors, teachers, schools, and factories in a couple of decades. Hard-won gains in agriculture and industry are more than wiped out by the increase in the number of mouths to feed. In many countries, children under the age of sixteen constitute one-half the population (as compared to one-quarter in countries with stable populations).

But the growth of population will also be disastrous in the United States since it contributes to urban blight and environmental pollution. Each American baby will in its lifetime directly or indirectly use 26 million

[33]Herbert Roback, "Do We Need a Department of Science and Technology?" *Science*, 165 (1969), 36; Donald F. Hornig, "United States Science Policy," *Science*, 163 (1969), 523; Harvey Brooks, *The Government of Science* (Cambridge, Mass.: The M.I.T. Press, 1968), Chap. 1.

gallons of water and 21,000 gallons of gasoline. We are using up irreplaceable minerals and raw materials taken from other countries as well as from our own. The quality of life is bound to deteriorate if current population trends are extrapolated (increases in urban congestion, juvenile delinquency, overcrowding, ecological devastation, etc.).

In such a situation, we cannot simply rely on ethical norms of the past. Overpopulation is a new and urgent problem never faced before in human history. The injunction in Genesis to "be fruitful and multiply" may have been sound advice to ancient Israel, but not to modern India or America. Some scientists think that the crisis is so desperate that only radical compulsory medical measures will be effective. One proposal calls for the compulsory sterilization of every woman after her second child. Several authors have recommended that a temporary sterilant be placed in water supplies. Or perhaps a lifelong contraceptive shot or time capsule could be given to every girl at the age of ten; the antidote that would neutralize it would be strictly controlled by the government. Permits for childbearing have been proposed—with a limit of two per couple if a stable population is to be maintained.

Now I would grant that in a crisis when its survival is at stake a society may have to qualify individual freedom. In an interdependent society, the freedom of one man—and another, and another—may eventually imperil every man's survival. "Rights" that have been taken as basic may have to be reevaluated under new conditions. The urgency of the global crisis does demand coercive measures. Overpopulation is an ominous threat to human dignity and fulfillment. Nevertheless some forms of coercion may be so repressive that they would also jeopardize human dignity. Compulsory measures that were strongly opposed by a populace could be enforced only by a regulatory bureaucracy that verged on police-state methods, endangering hard-won freedoms in other areas of life. The risks in manipulating human lives must enter our evaluation of compulsory medical measures.

Economic and social pressures, on the other hand, represent forms of coercion that avoid these dangers. At present, income tax deductions favor large families, but tax laws could be changed to allow deductions only for the first two children. There could be bonuses for each childless year, or for each family with no more than two children. Incentives might also be offered for every man offering voluntarily to undergo sterilization. Then again, social structures have a strong influence on family size. Birthrates could be lowered by increasing the minimum legal age for marriage and by making education and careers more widely available for young women. Parents in many societies want large families in order to have sons to support them in their old age; an adequate social security system providing old age insurance would fill this need without large families.

I would argue that voluntary contraception coupled with intensive education and economic and social incentives holds out real promise of significantly reducing bithrates. In the journal *Science*, Bernard Berelson, president of the Population Council, gives a detailed comparison of alternative proposals and defends the extension of existing family-planning programs; these already have considerable momentum, are widely accepted, and can be linked to maternal health and child care.[34] There is clear evidence that the poor in the United States do want to limit their family size. The obstacle to their use of family planning is not lack of motivation but the inaccessibility of medical services and the grossly unequal distribution of medical care in our society. In Louisiana the birthrate among low-income families fell 32 percent, and the illegitimacy rate 40 percent, in one year following the introduction of birth-control services in the state's clinics. Home visitation and follow-up were carried out by field workers recruited from the low-income groups themselves.

But it is not enough to prevent unwanted children through voluntary family planning. We must educate people to desire smaller families than they now wish. After all, the wanted child crowds and pollutes the earth as much as the unwanted child. We can appeal to fear by convincing people of the seriousness of the crisis; we can also appeal to self-interest and the advantages of small families. The life style of the small family must be legitimated, and the cultural images of family success transformed. A major worldwide program with massive funding administered through the United Nations is required, also a large corps of field workers, neighborhood and village clinics, a transistorized TV set in each village with transmissions from orbiting satellites, etc. There should be a much larger allocation of funds for research, especially on inexpensive, long-lasting contraceptive pills. Population control should be high on our national priorities—immediately. The time is now. While you have been reading this chapter, 10,000 babies have been born.

VI. CONCLUSIONS

I have proposed three strands in an interdisciplinary theology and ethic of ecology: man's unity with nature, God's immanence in nature, and responsible control of technology. I suggested that, despite the long-run importance of attitudes toward nature, the urgent demand is for political action in the name of human welfare and social justice. It would be appropriate to conclude with examples of the kinds of programs to which such an analysis might lead. There are, of course, many things that the individual can do—from cutting down on excessive consumption of goods to

---

[34]Bernard Berelson, "Beyond Family Planning," *Science*, 163 (1969), 533.

using biodegradable detergents and returnable bottles. But insofar as pollution is a product of the social uses of technology, it is a question for national policy and legislation.

1. Restraint in consumption. As individuals and groups we can make efforts to reduce excessive consumption and develop a style of life resistant to the pressures of an acquisitive society. This does not mean withdrawal from the world into ascetic otherworldliness, nor a romantic return to nature; to turn our backs on technology would condemn much of the world to degrading toil and abject poverty. But it does mean greater awareness of waste and deliberate action to conserve resources and re-cycle materials instead of discarding them. Moreover, as a nation we must reject the idea of an ever-increasing gross national product, and start the process of slowing down leading to a no-growth economy. We can no longer assume that resources are unlimited, or that someone will find a substitute when we run out. In the past, overall economic growth has benefited the poor, even though the relative distribution of wealth changed little; in a stable economy, the redistribution of wealth will be imperative, since it will be the main way of improving the lot of the poor.

2. The redirection of technology. In national policy, higher priority should be given to the abolition of hunger, poverty, and pollution, at home and abroad, than to the production of more luxury goods. Space and military technology are highly developed, but comparatively little effort has been given to the technology of urban housing, pollution abatement, or population control. We have the technical ability and the organizational skills to achieve a world from which are banished man's ancient enemies—war, disease, hunger, and poverty—as well as the new enemy—pollution. To this task the biblical tradition can bring a passion for social justice and equality, a prophetic concern for a more humane social order. The extreme inequalities of our society and our world cannot be allowed to continue. Technology must be used to reduce, not to increase, the gaps between the "haves" and "have nots," among individuals and among nations. The cru-cial challenge of this decade is the redirection of technology to the welfare of mankind. It demands a national dedication to our mutual survival comparable to the dedication mobilized in time of war, and a sense of urgency in the recognition that time is running out.

3. A Department of Environment. A separate department for en-vironmental protection is advisable, since when there is only one agency devoted to both developing a technology and protecting the public (e.g., the Atomic Energy Commission), the hazardous consequences have usually been underestimated. Without considerable independence an agency tends to be dominated by the industries it is supposed to regulate (e.g., the Federal Communication Commission). A cabinet-level Department of Environment would sponsor research and promote legislation on pollution reduction, environmental preservation, and consumer protection. It would include both natural and social scientists trained to study the effects of technological developments, in order to guide policy decisions and suggest legislation for the regulatory powers needed. It would collect ecological data and establish enforceable environmental standards. It would also conduct research on recycling procedures for reusing nonrenewable resuorces. We have to shift from a frontier mentality of using up and moving on, to a spaceship mentality of living on a fixed set of resources.

The image of the earth as a spaceship symbolizes both our finite resources and our global interdependence. On this frail planet we travel together to a common destiny; what one man does affects us all. The world is an ecosystem, a precarious habitat for all creatures. A universal society is struggling for birth, a society dedicated to the care of the earth and to the fulfillment of human existence within the kingdom of life of which we are a part—a society embodying a new awareness of the sanctity of life and a new responsibility for all creatures including those yet unborn. We are called both to the love of life and to the life of love. The picture of our spinning globe from 100,000 miles in space shows the incredible richness and beauty of our earth, a blue and white gem, a garden of Eden among the barren planets. Before it is too late, let us commit ourselves to keeping it habitable. We can yet act to fulfill the promise: "Earth shall be fair, and all her people one."